Wagner on Bands

Books by David Whitwell

Philosophic Foundations of Education
Foundations of Music Education
Music Education of the Future
The Sousa Oral History Project
The Art of Musical Conducting
The Longy Club: 1900–1917
A Concise History of the Wind Band

The History and Literature of the Wind Band and Wind Ensemble Series

www.whitwellbooks.com

David Whitwell

Wagner on Bands

Second Edition

Edited by Craig Dabelstein

Whitwell Books • Austin, Texas, USA

Wagner on Bands
Second Edition
Dr. David Whitwell
Edited by Craig Dabelstein
www.whitwellbooks.com

Whitwell Publishing
815-A Brazos Street #491
Austin, TX 78701
USA

Composed in Bembo
Published in the United States of America

Wagner on Bands (PAPERBACK) ISBN 978-1-936512-23-2

Foreword

WHEN I WAS A YOUNG STUDENT the name Wagner was not only common to the vocabulary of all musicians but was used as a hallmark, all things being said to be 'before Wagner' or 'after Wagner.' Toward the end of my career a chance comment in a rehearsal, followed by a question or two, brought to my attention that I had a room full of university students who had never heard a note of Wagner's music. I was astonished because his music had always seemed contemporary to me. One would not, for example, speak of 'performance practice in the music of Wagner.'

I had a similar experience as I was preparing to add some material to my little book, *Wagner on Bands* (1993). Looking over my notes I began to realize how much really valuable commentary there was in prose by Wagner on the subject of conducting. While his discussion seems very contemporary and deals with familiar problems, I suspect that much of what he discusses is little known to many band conductors today. Therefore, I have collected his thoughts into four essays and I am certain that they will stimulate much thinking by all readers. You will find you cannot 'speed read' these four essays, but they contain a great deal of wisdom which goes right to the heart of our profession.

I add one small topic here which has nothing to do with the book itself. It may come as a surprise to many readers that Wagner gave some thought to coming to America, like Napoleon before him (who missed the boat) and Maelzel (who died in America). On 5 July 1848 Wagner wrote to Löbmann, the Kapellmeister in Riga:

> I, for my part, tell you frankly that if I were a poor performing musician I would not go to America now, for the simple reason that I should have been there long ago. What slavery is the lot of us poor musicians over here! I can see no grounds for dissuading any one from seeking his fortune there, where he is more likely to find it under any circumstances than here.

Due to the fast growing population, Wagner goes on to suggest that even entire orchestras might consider emigrating together. And in fact I can think of at least one fine Italian civic band which did exactly that early in the twentieth century.

In September 1849, Wagner tells his friend, the singer Heine, that only the unfinished Ring cycle prevents him from going.

> If it comes to the worst I shall write to my patron, your Wilhelm, in America, and tell him to get me some kind of post, as the last of the German Mohicans; then you shall pack us up with you and we will all sail together. If I still hold on with all my roots in Europe, it is because I have work to do here, and with all my mind's weapons.

Five years later, in January 1854, Wagner writes Liszt:

> While I live here like a beggar, I hear from America that in Boston they are already giving 'Wagner nights.' Some one implores me to come; he says that interest in me is rapidly growing there; that I could make much money with concert performances, etc.

The following year Wagner had a firm offer to come for six months of conducting in New York. The money was sufficient to be tempting, but having recently had an extended visit conducting in London which was less than fulfilling, Wagner hesitated. Eventually he wrote his contact saying that if the Ring prospects did not soon improve he would 'have his scores neatly bound, put on a shelf and go to America.' Given that choice, we are glad he stayed home.

David Whitwell
Austin, Texas

Contents

Acknowledgments

The reader is indebted for the second edition of this book to Mr. Craig Dabelstein. Without his creative ideas, contribution to design and all things involved as an editor this book would never again have been available.

David Whitwell
Austin, 2011

Part 1

Wagner on the Conductor and Conducting

Wagner on the Conductor as a Man

Music is the speech of Passion.[1]

The Musician addresses himself to the Feeling, and not to the Understanding. If he be answered in terms of the Understanding, then it is as good as said that he has not been understood …

Criticism is nothing else than the avowal of the misunderstanding of the composition, which can only be really understood by the Feeling.[2]

These two observations by Richard Wagner are understood by every thoughtful conductor. They are at the heart of problems the conductor faces at every rehearsal: he feels he knows what the composer intended, but to communicate this to the ensemble if he chooses to do this through language then, exactly as Wagner says, there is a good chance he will be misunderstood. And, in his duty to communicate a composer's most private feelings to a public that has little or no rational knowledge of music he cannot risk using technical language at all.

This fundamental paradox which the conductor faces has been made clear to us today through the past forty years of clinical brain research. Basically the experiential part of music, the feelings, are in the right hemisphere of the brain while the rational aspects of music, notation and grammar (theory), are in the left hemisphere, as appropriate to that library of rational understanding. Wagner did not have this advantage which makes things so clear to us, but like many thinkers before him he arrived at the basic idea on his own. So when Wagner used 'understanding' versus 'feeling,' as he did in the above quotation, he was right on the mark for describing left hemisphere and right hemisphere and in his writings we can trace to some degree the development of his thoughts.

When Wagner writes, 'Music is the beginning and end of Language,'[3] he refers both to the belief among nearly all philologists today that musical sounds, based on the vowels, were a form of communication long before language as we know it and, on the other extreme, that music expresses those things which language cannot. It follows, he believed, that Feeling is

[1] Richard Wagner, 'Judaism in Music, in Richard Wagner, *Richard Wagner's Prose Works*, trans. William Ashton Ellis (New York: Broude Brothers, 1966), 3:86.

[2] 'A Communication to my Friends,' in ibid., 1:271. I have substituted the English synonyms for two of Wagner's sometimes obscure German, for example his constant use of 'art work' to mean a composition.

[3] 'Opera and Drama,' vol. 2, chap. 6, in ibid., 2:224.

the beginning and end of Understanding. This also seems true as we feel before we can explain and after all explanations it is feeling which determines our choices.

The reader can see the potential confusion which arises from this result of our evolution. Wagner, in the following, traces how in becoming left-brain oriented we have lost touch with feeling. This is critical because the feeling side of us, the right brain, is the real us. So one might say that in agreeing to the conformity of society we have lost self and we no longer speak a language which is rooted in our individual experience.

> The Understanding, condensed from Feeling through the Imagination [Phantasy], acquired in Prosaic word-speech an organ through which it could make itself intelligible *alone*, and in direct ratio as it became un-intelligible to Feeling. In modern Prose we speak a language we do not understand with the Feeling, since its connection with the objects, whose impression on our faculties first ruled the molding of the speech-roots, has become incognizable to us; a language which we speak as it was taught us in our youth,—not as, with waxing self-dependence of our Feeling, we haply seize, form, and feed it from ourselves and the objects we behold; a language whose usages and claims, based on the logic of the Understanding, we must unconditionally obey when we want to impart our thoughts.[4]

'In a sense, we cannot discourse in this language according to our innermost emotion.' Wagner is correct about this, as in the example of the futility in trying to write an adequate love letter, even though he lacked the advantage we have in understanding that in fact the Understanding and the Feeling are really separate functions. Lacking this knowledge, he speculated on man's evolution and concluded that it was because early man could not express his feelings through language that, 'therefore in our modern evolution it was altogether consequent that the Feeling should have sought a refuge ... by fleeing to absolute tone-speech, our Music of today.'[5]

For these reasons, Wagner felt a strong sympathy with the poet, the artist who must depend on left brain communication and the barrier that represents. The poet must translate his feelings into language in such a way that he leads the reader from language back to feeling. 'The poet's aim,' Wagner writes, 'is never realized until it passes from the Understanding to the Feeling.'[6] It follows, as part of his argument for

4 Ibid., 2:230.

5 Ibid., 2:231.

6 Ibid., 2:232.

the music drama, that the poet can only communicate feeling convincingly, 'through the primal organ of the soul's inner feeling—through music.'[7]

A great turning point for Wagner occurred when in 1854 he was introduced to the philosophical literature of Schopenhauer, who at last gave him a deeper understanding about the nature of Reason versus Feeling.[8] With the cultural interest in Germany in the forthcoming of the hundredth birthday of Beethoven in 1870 Wagner began to think about the great universality of Beethoven's music and, in turn, about the nature of man and music. One most important aspect of Wagner's discussion is that it offers a glimpse into what was meant by that all-important word, *melos*, which Wagner coined to represent the core understanding of a composer's music needed by the conductor or performer.

Schopenhauer was one of the first who wrote at length on the bicameral nature of man, however, he reached the conclusion that the separation comes from the perspective of either looking out from ourselves or looking inward. Wagner paraphrases this as follows:

> If we couple with this what Schopenhauer postulates as the condition for entry of an Idea into our consciousness, namely 'a temporary preponderance of intellect over will, or to put it physiologically, a strong excitation of the sensory faculty of the brain without the smallest excitation of the passions or desires,' we have only further to pay close heed to the elucidation which directly follows it, namely that our consciousness has two sides: in part it is a consciousness of one's own self, which is the will; in part a consciousness of other things, and chiefly then a visual knowledge of the outer world, the apprehension of objects. 'The more the one side of the aggregate consciousness comes to the front, the more does the other retreat.'

As Wagner correctly observed, Schopenhauer was one of the first philosophers who clearly understood that music was fundamentally different from the other arts. We do not observe and appreciate music as we do a sculpture, for example. Music gets inside us, a reality which was at the heart of Aristotle's creation of the concept of catharsis. Further, Schopenhauer was fascinated by the essential paradox of music, that it cannot be strictly explained in any logical terms and yet it is immediately understood by everyone. It was for this rea-

[7] Ibid. 2:233.

[8] The following discussion by Wagner is found in 'Beethoven,' in ibid., 5:64ff. Schopenhauer's writings on music are highly recommended above all other nineteenth-century philosophers for the reader who has the time and mood for reflection on music and its relationship to the basic nature of man.

son that Schopenhauer concluded that Music was not merely something to be learned but rather, '*Music is itself an Idea of the world.*' This conclusion cannot be separated from the idea that music includes significant genetic information, something which has been substantiated by clinical research and which is the basis of the maxim, 'Music is the Universal Language.'

Wagner paraphrases Schopenhauer's presentation of these last ideas in the following passage. The reader should pay particular attention to Schopenhauer's conclusion that music cannot be understood through objective knowledge. With respect to the conductor this truth is the basis of why we do not arrive at an understanding of a score through traditional objective analysis of the grammar of the composition.

> We should not understand [Music's] character itself were not the inner essence of things confessed to us elsewhere, dimly at least and in our Feeling. For that essence cannot be gathered from the Ideas, nor understood through any mere *objective* knowledge; wherefore it would ever remain a mystery, had we not access to it from quite another side.
>
> Only inasmuch as every observer is an Individual withal, and thereby part of Nature, stands there open to him in his own self-consciousness the path to Nature's innermost; and there forthwith, and most immediately, it makes itself known to him as *Will*.

It seems clear that *melos* had much to do with that in music which is of the nature of man, of an interior sense and of communication through feeling. One finds this, as Wagner makes clear, through 'inner vision' or 'facing inwards,' in Schopenhauer's words. Only here, contends Wagner, 'can the intellect derive its ability to seize the Character of things.'

Wagner summarizes the special universal nature of music and its *melos* in an important passage.

> Music, who speaks to us solely through quickening into articulate life the most universal concept of the inherently speechless Feeling, in all imaginable gradations, can once and for all be judged by nothing but the category of the *sublime*; for, as soon as she engrosses us, she transports us to the highest ecstasy of consciousness of our infinitude.
>
> On the other hand what enters only *as a sequel* to our plunging into contemplation of a work of plastic art, namely the (temporary) liberation of the intellect from service to the individual will through our discarding all relations of the object contemplated to that will—the required effect of *beauty* on the mind—is brought about by Music at her

very *first entry*; inasmuch as she withdraws us at once from any concert with the relation of things outside us, and—as pure Form set free from Matter—shuts us off from the outer world, as it were, to let us gaze into the inmost Essence of ourselves and all things.

Consequently our verdict on any piece of music should be based upon a knowledge of those laws whereby the effect of Beauty, the very first effect of Music's mere appearance, advances the most directly to a revelation of her truest character through the agency of the Sublime. It would be the stamp of an absolutely empty piece of music, on the contrary, that it never got beyond a mere prismatic toying with the effect of its first entry, and consequently kept us bound to the relations presented by Music's outermost side to the world of vision.

Let us emphasize the final sentence: the mark of a poor composition is if it is merely beautiful, but never draws the listener to inner contemplation, and if the composition only draws us to its 'outermost side,' its grammar or theory. Wagner returns to this later saying that it is 'a great misapprehension of [music's] character' if we are only concerned in 'our pleasure in beautiful forms,' or mere beauty. This reminds us of the great conductor Celebadache's observation that whoever speaks of the Beauty of music does not understand music.

Wagner also adds a warning that has to do with the concept of programmatic music. Since music does not 'portray the Ideas inherent in the world's phenomena,' but rather inner things, it is questionable whether music can in fact ever be anything else but music. The conductor or performer must, therefore, give extra thought to any piece with an inviting descriptive title.

Finally, let us stress that in the above quotation Wagner certainly identifies the most important characteristic of music, both for performers, listeners and for its application in education, when he wrote,

> Music lets us gaze into the inmost Essence of ourselves.

He was thinking of this at the conclusion of an essay on Beethoven.

> As Christianity stepped forth amid the Roman civilization of the universe, so Music breaks forth from the chaos of modern civilization. Both say aloud: 'our kingdom is not of this world.' And that means: we come from within, ye from without; we spring from the Essence of things, ye from their Show.

In another place, Wagner gives his famous definition of music, 'Music lets us gaze into the inmost Essence of ourselves,' a broader application, 'Music is the revelation of the inner vision of the Essence of the World.'[9] One can see again the influence also of Schopenhauer in Wagner's attention to Nature and the Inner Man.

9 'Beethoven,' in ibid., 5:108.

Wagner begins his most famous treatise, 'The Art-Work of the Future,' with a discussion he calls 'Nature, Man and Art.' His first sentence, 'As Man stands to Nature, so stands Art to Man,' has its significance to Wagner in the importance of man to recognize and express 'Nature's *Necessity*.' He expands on this idea in the following and, as he was a conductor himself, there can be little doubt that he would have associated this definition perfectly with the relationship of conducting motions to the music one feels inside and not to what one sees on paper. Further, while he admits that face and arm can express emotions, the feelings of the true inner man can only be expressed by the nature of the music he makes.

> Man will never be that which he can and should be, until his Life is a true mirror of Nature, a conscious following of the only real Necessity, the *inner natural necessity*, and is no longer held in subjugation to an *outer* artificial counterfeit [notation].[10]

10 'The Art-Work of the Future,' in ibid., 1:71

This discussion Wagner follows with his basic definition of the inner and outer man.

> Man's nature is twofold, an *outer* and an *inner*. The senses by which he offers himself to the observer as a subject for Art, are those of *Vision* and of *Hearing*: to the eye appeals the outer man, the inner to the ear ...
>
> The corporeal man and the spontaneous expression of his sensations of physical anguish or well-being [happiness], called up by outward contact, appeal directly to the eye, while indirectly he imparts to it, by means of facial play and gesture, those emotions of the inner man which are not directly understood by the (observer's) eye ... The more distinctly can the outer man express the inner, the higher does he show his rank as an artistic being.
>
> But the inner man can only find *direct* communication through the ear, and that by means of *his voice's music*. Music is the immediate utterance of feeling ... Through the sense of hearing, music urges forth from the feeling of one heart to the feeling of [another].[11]

11 'The Art-Work of the Future,' in ibid., 1:91

In another place Wagner stresses this vital concept:

> Everything lives and lasts by the inner Necessity of its being, by its own nature's Need. It lay in the nature of the art of music to evolve herself to a capability of the most definite and manifold expression [of that which] lay hid within her soul.[12]

[12] 'Opera and the Nature of Music,' part 1, in ibid., 2:35.

Finally, before leaving the general topic of 'Understanding versus Feeling,' and the fundamental challenge it poses for the conductor, Wagner has left us not only a testimonial to the influence of the above ideas on him, but once more to something very meaningful to him: the conductor will not understand these explanations in the realm of separate brain functions, on the inner versus the outer man or on the awareness of the role of inner Necessity unless they correspond with things he has *already* found within himself.

> I have come to interpret the problem of differentiating between intuitions and concepts—a problem resolved for me by Schopenhauer's profound and happy solution—not simply as a conception but as an experience, the truth of which has now impressed itself upon me with such compelling conviction that, especially now that I have admitted to myself the true nature of the situation, I am perfectly content to accept it for myself and not be misled into presuming to force it upon others by a process of dialectic reasoning. I myself recognize all too well that such a conviction could never have been forced upon me if it had not already corresponded to my own deepest intuitions; equally, I recognize that it cannot be forced upon anyone else wither, unless he has grasped it intuitively before he recognizes its conceptual validity. We cannot accept a thing conceptually if we have not already grasped it intuitively: this state of affairs is too self-evident for anyone who has seen it clearly for himself especially if he feels as little of a philosopher as I do, to expose himself in public as a dialectician. I can speak only in [in music].

Another subject which Wagner discussed and which is familiar to every conductor today is the role of society, and particularly government, and the arts. He was familiar with the writings of the ancient Greek philosophers and he found the education of the Greek, from his earliest youth, made him the subject of his own artistic treatment and enjoyment, in body as in spirit.[13] He then traces the lack of freedom during the following centuries from the Church (who only promised a better next life) to the aristocracy which held musicians as slaves.

[13] This, and the following discussion, is found in 'Art and Revolution,' in ibid., 1:46ff.

Wagner claims that Napoleon told Goethe that the role of Fate in the ancient world had, since Roman times, become Politics. The result, as is obvious to all educators today, is a gearing of everything by the State to the middle, if not the lowest, part of society. The individual is shackled to mediocrity and,

> more open to arbitrary interpretings, in the *ethical views of society* by which the instinctive impulse of the State-included Individual is finally influenced or judged. The life-bent of the Individual utters itself forever *newly* and *directly*, but the essence of Society is use and wont and its 'view' a *mediated* one. Wherefore the 'view' of Society, so long as it does not fully comprehend the essence of the Individual and its own genesis therefrom, is a hindering and a shackling one and becomes ever more tyrannical in exact degree as the quickening and innovating essence of the Individual brings it instinctive thrust to battle against habit.[14]

[14] This discussion begins with the final paragraph of 'Opera and Drama,' part 2, in ibid., vol. 2.

Today as a result, Wagner contends that the very idea of the Individual outside of society is completely unthinkable by us.[15] The State, however,

[15] 'Opera and Drama', part 2, 'The Play and the Nature of Dramatic Poetry,' chap. 4.

> is a stiff, dogmatic, fettering and domineering might, which lays down for the individual in advance, 'So shalt thou think and deal!' The State has assumed the education of the individual's character; it takes possession of him already in the mother's womb, through foreordaining him an unequal share in the means toward social self-dependence …
>
> The citizen is impotent to take a single step which is not set down for him in advance, as wither a *duty* or a *crime*. The character of his duty and his crime is not one proper to his individuality. Let him try as he may, to act upon his never so free thinking, yet he cannot step outside the State—to whom even his crime belong. Only through *death* can he cease to be a citizen of the State; thus only where he also ceases to be a human being.

Today, Wagner concludes, you are only free if you have money. So,

> we must not be astonished that Art grasps after gold; for everything strives to its freedom, towards its god, and our god is Gold, our religion the Pursuit of Wealth.

He warns, also, that government always supports arts for the wrong reason, as for example the government's reopening the theaters after the mid-nineteenth century revolutions, not for the sake of art but to calm the passions of the public, to absorb their excitement and 'divert the threatening agitation of the heated public mind.'

In the same way, the government supports education for only the most commercial purposes.

> Our foolish education, fashioned for the most part to fit us merely for future industrial gain 'forces us to seek the subjects of any kind of artistic amusement outside ourselves—like the rake who goes for the fleeting joys of love to the arms of a prostitute.'

He finds this kind of education produces not an artist free to achieve the highest aesthetic goals of his art, but rather a kind of artist–mechanic, one whose sights are on the rewards of society and the state.

> The *true artist* finds delight not only in the aim of his creation, but also in the very process of creation, in the handling and molding of his material. The very act of production is to him a gladsome, satisfying activity, not toil.
>
> The *journeyman* reckons only the goal of his labor, the profit which his toil shall bring him. The energy which he expends gives him no pleasure, it is but a fatigue, and inevitable task, a burden which he would gladly give over to a machine. His toil is but a fettering chain. For this reason, he is never present with his work in spirit …[16]
>
> He is a Slave of Industry and our modern factories afford us the sad picture of the deepest degradation of man, constant labor, killing both body and soul, without joy or love, often almost without aim.

In a letter to a friend Wagner is even more pessimistic.

> That I ever set store by the workers as workers is something I must now atone for grievously: with the noises they make, these workers are the most wretched slaves, whom anyone can control nowadays if he promises them plenty of 'work.' A slave mentality has taken root in everything with us: that we are *human* is something nobody knows in the whole of France![17]

[16] When I first read this I had the uncomfortable feeling that Wagner was describing my first year of conducting in which I followed the only model I had, my university band director. I had been trained to think of the rehearsal as a place for unrelenting hard work, followed by an occasional concert at which time music was finally rewarding. An older music educator asked me about this and commented that he always enjoyed the rehearsals as much as the concert because 'it is still a time for making music.' This changed my life, for until that moment I had never thought of the rehearsal as a time for music making. In my university band the rehearsal was not a time for music making; it was a period of severe psychological intimidation. And like that mysterious figure, Punjab, who followed Daddy Warbucks around in the old Little Orphan Annie cartoon strip, my university band director could make people disappear. I recall a rehearsal when a graduate student was running a bit late and was seated but still looking for the first composition of the rehearsal as the band director was ready to begin. The director made a nasty remark about the student not being ready and the student replied, 'Just give me a second, Chief, and I'll be with you!' Since the band director never encouraged any form of question, or any comment directed to him in rehearsal, he took this as disrespectful. At the next rehearsal the graduate was missing, his chair filled by someone new. Not only had he thus disappeared from the band, but he had disappeared from the School of Music. No one ever saw him again!

[17] Letter to Ernst Kietz in Paris, Dec. 30, 1851, in John N. Burk, *Letters of Richard Wagner* (New York: Vienna House, 1972), 243.

In spite of this environment, Art remains in its essence what it ever was, contends Wagner. The main difference is that with the ancient Greeks, 'Art lived in the public conscience, whereas today it lives alone in the conscience of private persons.' The public is not only '*un*-conscience to Art,' but assigns it no significance. And it was because of this separation of society and art that Wagner observed, 'The severance of the Artist from the Man is as brainless an attempt as the divorce of the soul from the body.'[18]

Wagner makes the basic argument that if we wish to advance the case of the individual against the State the argument must be addressed to *feeling* and not an appeal to the Understanding. But to do this the artist today is basically a 'revolutionary, because his very existence is opposed to the ruling spirit of the community.' Furthermore, since the values of the artist come from within and are experiential, it makes it very difficult to make the individuals who represent the State understand.

> That which is most unique to us as individuals we owe not to our conceptualizations but to our intuitions: but these latter are so much our own that we can never fully express them nor adequately communicate them, for even the most complete attempt to do so, which is what the artist does in his art, is ultimately apprehended by others, in turn, purely in accordance with their own particular way of apprehending things.[19]

Finally, we offer an interesting commentary by Wagner on music and society of his generation, one reflecting a frequent topic in early philosophy—the influence of geography and climate on man. He offers it as a way of suggesting that it is the German musician who best represents the highest aesthetic purpose.

> Somebody once said: The Italian uses music for love, the Frenchman for society, but the German a science. Perhaps it would be better put: The Italian is a singer, the Frenchman a virtuoso, the German a musician.
>
> The German has a right to be styled by the exclusive name 'Musician,' for of him one may say that he loves Music for herself—not as a means of charming, of winning gold and admiration, but because he worships her as a divine and lovely art that, if he gives himself to her, becomes his one and all. The German is capable of writing music merely for himself and friend, uncaring if it will ever be executed for a public.[20]

[18] 'A Communication to my Friends,' in Wagner, *Richard Wagner's Prose Works*, trans. Ellis, 1:270.

[19] Letter to August Röckel, August 23, 1856 from Zurich, in Burk, *Letters of Richard Wagner*, 356.

[20] 'On German Music,' in Wagner, *Richard Wagner's Prose Works*, trans. Ellis, 7:85.

Wagner on the Education of the Conductor

It is necessary to have a teacher who by his teaching and precepts stirs
and awakens the moral virtues whose seed is enclosed and buried in our
souls and who, like a good farmer, cultivates and clears the way for them
by removing the thorns and tares of our appetites which often so darken
and choke our minds.

Baldassare Castiglione, 1478–1529[1]

In the previous essay, 'Wagner on the Conductor as a Man,'
we have quoted some of his thoughts on how society, including education, seeks to shape everyone toward some middle
point, thus ignoring the importance of the individual and
subsequently by definition the arts. One of his chief objections
with respect to State control of education was that its fundamental goal was simply to prepare people for industrial gain
and to teach people to just exist, to get through life.

> The crime and the curse of our social intercourse have lain in this: that
> the mere physical maintenance of life has been till now the one object
> of our *care*—a real *care* that has devoured our souls and bodies and well
> nigh lamed each spiritual impulse. This *Care* has made man weak and
> slavish, dull and wretched; a creature that can neither love nor hate; a
> thrall of commerce, ever ready to give up the last vestige of the freedom
> of his Will, so only that this *Care* might be a little lightened.[2]

Wagner bemoans the fact that the effect of this kind of educational philosophy that includes even the teaching of art
as commerce, how to make a living, has a deadly impact on
art itself.

> What has revolted the architect, when he must shatter his creative force
> on bespoken plans for barracks and lodging-houses? What has aggrieved
> the painter, when he must immortalize the repugnant face of a mil-
> lionaire? What the musician, when he must compose his music for the
> banquet table? And what the poet, when he must write romances for
> the lending-library?
>
> What then has been the sting of suffering to each? That he must
> squander his creative powers for gain, and make his art a handicraft![3]

[1] Baldassare Castiglione, *Il Cortigiano*,
trans., George Bull (New York: Penguin
Books, 1967), 3:291.

[2] 'Art and Revolution,' in Wagner,
Richard Wagner's Prose Works, 1:57.

[3] 'Art and Revoltion,' in ibid., 1:61

Wagner offers as an antidote, for a State educational philosophy which discounts the individual, a focus on the universality of Feeling and the key which this offers as well for the individual.

> But Feeling only grasps the akin to itself; just as the naked Understanding can only parley with the Understanding. The Feeling stays cold amid the reflections of the Understanding: only the reality of an object kindred to itself can warm it into interest. This object must be the sympathetic image of the instinctive doer's own nature; and sympathetically it can only work when it displays itself in an action vindicated by the self-same feeling which, from out of this action and this vindication, he fellow-feels (*mitfühlt*) as his very own. Through this fellow-feeling he just as instinctively attains an understanding of his own individual nature, as by the objects and opposites of his feeling and dealing—by whose contact his own feeling-and-dealing had evolved itself, in the image—he has also learnt the nature of those opposites; and this because, snatched out of himself by lively sympathy for his own likeness, he is carried on to take instinctive interest in the feelings and dealings even of his opposites, is tuned to acknowledgment of, and the justice toward these opposites, since they no longer stand confronting the bias of his actual dealings.

Wagner goes even further, suggesting that by engaging Society through Feeling, Feeling itself can influence the observer's Understanding, which he calls *emotionalizing of the intellect*. While modern clinical brain studies find things to challenge here, certainly Wagner's following basic premise is very true.

> The Understanding tells us: '*So it is*,' only when the Feeling has told us: '*So it must be*.' Only through *itself*, however does this Feeling become intelligible to itself: it understands no other language than its own. Things which can only be explained to us by the infinite accommodations of the Understanding, embarrass and confound the Feeling.[4]

4 'Opera and Drama,' part 2, chap. 4, in ibid., 2:209.

In a following section, 'Opera and Drama,' part 2, chapter 6, we discover the premise upon which Wagner builds his conviction that Feeling can impact Understanding. It is here that he discusses his belief, one shared by a number of early philosophers and nearly all philologists today, that music came before speech in early man—that man first communicated through musical-like pitches, basically the vowel sounds, thus lending a new level of universality to his argument.

In these vowels, if we think of them as stripped of their consonants, and picture to ourselves the manifold and vivid play of inner feelings, with all their range of joy and sorrow, as given out in them alone, we shall obtain an image of man's first emotional language; a language in which the stirred and high-strung Feeling could certainly express itself through nothing but a [joining together of these] ringing tones, which altogether in itself must take on the appearance of Melody.

Another goal which Wagner would have wished could be re-introduced to educational philosophy, one no doubt he gained from his reading of the works of the ancient Greek philosophers, was character formation, in particular manners. While philosophers supported this purpose in music education for two thousand years, by Wagner's lifetime interest in the subject was falling rapidly. He mentions this in passing in the course of discussing a formal paper he wrote in 1846 in Dresden in which he argued for the creation of a special conservatory for performers.

Music is able to work on taste, yes, also upon *manners*. The first point will be disputed by no one, even in our day, but a direct relation to morality has not as yet been generally ascribed to Music, in fact it has even been judged as morally quite harmless. That is not so. Could an effeminate and frivolous taste remain without influence on a man's morality? Both go hand in hand, and act reciprocally upon each other. Leaving aside the Spartans, who forbade a certain type of music as injurious to morals, let us think back to our own immediate past. With tolerable certainty we may contend that those inspired by *Beethoven's* music have been more active and energetic citizens-of-State than those bewitched by Rossini, Bellini and Donizetti, a class consisting for the most part of rich and lordly do-nothings.

Further proof is afforded by Paris. Anyone might have observed during the last decades that in exact degree as the morals of Parisian society have rushed into that unexampled corruption, its music has floundered in a sphere of frivolous taste. One has only to hear the latest compositions of an Auber or Adam and to compare them with the odious dances performed in Paris at the time of Carnival to perceive a terrible connection.[5]

[5] Ibid., 7:355.

His proposal for the special conservatory was very interesting in other respects as well.[6] The care and thought which Wagner gave to this proposal is evident in the letter which accompanied its submission to the intendant of the court orchestra.

[6] This can be found under 'A National Theatre,' in ibid., 7:354. The plan was rejected a year later, in 1847.

I have spent the last three months, taking the greatest pains, in subjecting everything I thought necessary to the strictest and most exact scrutiny, carefully weighing every point, leading to the revision and rewriting of some paragraphs two, three and even four times, and have now at last completed the enclosed work, in respect of which I beg to assure Your Excellency that I have not been motivated by any ulterior consideration.[7]

[7] Quoted in Curt von Westernhagen, *Wagner* (London: Cambridge University Press, 1978), 1:90.

There are a number of interesting details in this document, such as an ideal orchestral seating plan ('the width should never be more than twice the depth') and the interesting revelation that one of the court double bass players was required to also play tuba. Wagner urged this man's pay be increased, 'because he needs the best nourishment possible to give him the strength.'

Wagner, for political reasons since there was already a Conservatoire in Leipzig, did not go into much detail at this time but it is clear that the school he wanted to form in Dresden was to be entirely performance oriented. His suggestion on how the functions of the two schools might be organized is rather enlightening.

> The balance between the public functions of the two cities might accordingly be thus adjusted: *Leipzig* is the center of the *scientific* education [in music] for the country through its University; *Dresden* the focus of *artistic* education through its union of the Conservatorium with the National Institute for Drama and Music [which he argued the creation of].

In other words, Wagner proposes a plan here which takes us right back to the medieval separation of *musica speculativa* and *musica practica*, a separation which lurks behind the organization of all music schools yet today.

We are fortunate in the case of Wagner to have something quite rare among major composers: lengthy views on university music education. All music educators will recall that the purpose of music education among the ancient Greeks was primarily for the purpose of character development. When the Church won the contest against Rome all this changed dramatically. The Church, of course, took over the responsibility of character development for itself and closed the schools. Because the Church wanted to eliminate emotions[8] from

[8] St. Basil said a good Christian should not even laugh, since laughing is a form of emotion.

the lives of the new Christians, when schools were reopened music was admitted only under the slight of hand by making music part of the field of mathematics. As one can imagine, no one outside of Church loyalist could accept this logic and so the Church struck a new bargain, which we have mentioned above: the schools would teach 'paper' music, *musica speculativa*, (theory, composition and history) and everything having to do with performance, *musica practica*, would be left to the musicians out in the street to teach.

Today, one thousand five hundred years later, this division is still with us. Not only can its shadow be seen in many university music departments, but some universities still specialize in the 'paper,' or non-performance aspects of music. I once heard a professor at one of these universities issue the following cultural dogma: The study of Clarinet is to Music Literature as the study of Typing is to English Literature.

There is one small problem which the academics have, in their self-interest, overlooked for one thousand five hundred years: the 'paper' part is not music. Music only exists in performance heard by a listener; the paper part is mere data entirely located in the left hemisphere of the brain.

With this background the reader will understand that when Wagner was asked by Ludwig II to prepare recommendations for the creation of a state music school in Munich, he envisioned a music school which taught music: performance and performance practice. The reader will notice that over and over again Wagner contends that performance is the vehicle for music education and that the performance must always have as its aim Feeling.

Wagner begins his essay on music schools with the popular European title, Conservatory. What, he asks, are we conserving? As he will later make clear, what he thinks the conservatories should conserve is performance practice. He finds Italy and France do this,[9] but not the German-speaking countries. Because this has been lacking in a disciplined way, he saw the recent history as one which began with individual artists who filled their programs with whatever was available to fill up an evening.[10] The popularity of the Oratorio tradition in England he attributes more to religious aspects than musical ones. Even the nineteenth-century tradition of German Music Festivals he found marred by poor aesthetic taste.

[9] I once heard a European demand that Americans should not play European music since we know nothing about it.

[10] The premiere of Beethoven's 7th Symphony in Vienna shared the program with a mechanical trumpet player.

By the side of more solid art delights, the public notwithstanding pays its eager visits to the worst stage-performances of the vilest genre of Opera; also that, immediately before or after a symphony by Mozart or Beethoven, the most nonsensical behavior of a virtuoso, the most trivial aria of a *prima donna*, could win applause, nay, rouse enthusiasm.[11]

[11] 'A Music School for Munich,' in Wagner, *Richard Wagner's Prose Works*, 4:190.

The fact that the concert halls are frequently filled by an innocent public seeking 'harmless entertainment' deludes the concert planners into thinking they are providing an important service. The works of the great masters have thus, according to Wagner, influenced the public through the verdicts of the authorities, rather than 'through a genuine impression on the Feeling.'[12] This, he says, is because we (the Germans) 'possess classical works, but as yet no classic interpretation for them.'

[12] Ibid., 191.

Again he mentions the great care that foreign cities give in learning the (foreign) German repertoire. And it is true, in the middle of the ninetenth century the best orchestra in Paris rehearsed Beethoven's *Ninth Symphony* for three years before performing it before the public. They could have played, of course, after one rehearsal, but it was understanding the music which was their concern.

How different Wagner finds Germany. To illustrate his concern, he takes the example of Mozart.

Let anyone name me the school in Germany where the authentic interpretation of Mozart's music has been established and preserved! Does this knowledge come to our orchestras and their conductors absolutely by itself? But who has ever taught them?

Take the very simplest instance, the instrumental works of Mozart … and you shall see here two things: their great claims upon a singable interpretation and the scanty indications in the scores bequeathed to us. We know how hurriedly Mozart wrote down the score of a Symphony, for mere purpose of one particular performance at a concert he was just about to give. And on the other hand, how peremptory he was with regard to the expression of its song-like melodies when he rehearsed it with the orchestra. Everything here, you see, was reckoned for the direct communion of the master with his orchestra. In the parts it therefore sufficed to mark the principal tempo, with simple specifications of *forte* and *piano* for whole periods, because the master could dictate to the orchestra members the interpretation he wanted for his melodies, actually singing them for the most part. Even today, albeit we have accustomed ourselves to a most minute notation of the nuances of phrasing, the more talented conductor often finds himself obliged to teach his ensemble members very weighty, but delicate shadings of expression by *vivâ voce* explanation; and these communications, as a rule, are better understood and heeded, than the written signs.[13]

We must pause here for two comments. First, if Wagner knew one or more seventy-year-old musicians while he was working in Dresden, it was very possible that he knew someone who had actually been present when Mozart rehearsed one of his works in Vienna. Therefore we must regard the details here, Mozart's demands regarding expression, his singing the melodies to the orchestra, etc., as possibly being rare and important insights into Mozart's own work as a conductor.

Second, we must point out that even today music schools do not emphasize performance practice, rather they leave it to the student who knows nothing of the subject. Moreover, I can say generally that university band directors are not interested in this subject. Each of them seems to think, as Wagner suggests above, that somehow by magic they know how to perform Mozart. Most of them assert they understand Mozart, while they then turn around and make him sound like Brahms.

Wagner returns to the emphasis on feeling when he begins to concentrate on the curriculum of the new school. The school must make it understood to the students that it is the 'extraordinary feeling' that distinguishes Mozart from Haydn. And when it comes to Bach where Wagner admits the authentic interpretation may never be known, nevertheless the goal of the school must be to make the works of Bach 'entirely understandable to Feeling.'[14]

> I must commence by referring once more to the essential watchful care of the proposed Music school, which can be of profit only when it rigidly confines its work to fostering the art of interpretation.

For the areas of theory and composition he seems to suggest that the school only 'prescribe the main lines for his purely technical learning of the tools of music' and then send the student off (outside the school) to the best opportunity to learn actual composition.

> The invisible bond, uniting the various branches of instruction, will always have to be to attend to interpretation. And for interpretation, then, not only must one mature the performers themselves, but above all the aesthetic taste, the self-reliant judgment of the Right and Beautiful.

And this, he emphasizes, cannot be pursued through abstract scientific paths, or academic lectures, and the like, but 'here, too, we must strike the purely practical path of direct artistic exercise, under higher guidance for the interpretation.' At the end of the period of studies he suggests one might have academic lectures on Aesthetics of music, but,

> the history of music we must teach in no other way but by beautiful and correct performances of works of classical music.[15]

[15] Ibid., 199ff.

This reference to music history leads Wagner naturally to the question of the performance of early music. One problem which bothered Wagner was the juxtaposition on a concert program of 'wayward assortments of works of the most diverse style.' He points to a program he heard in which Bach, Mozart and then Rossini (Overture to *William Tell*) was heard. I think what bothered Wagner most was the audience's 'boisterous applause' for the Rossini. We have written in another place of this problem, that ending with a 'popular' work tends to erase the memory of the earlier compositions and leaves the audience with the impression they had attended an entertainment event. Nevertheless, most conductor's today would consider what Wagner and I are opposed to as being merely good programming.

The other problem with performing early music was that Wagner had the opinion that no one knew the performance practice of earlier periods. We enjoy the advantage today of having numerous memoirs, treatises and teaching methods from earlier periods which contain much valuable contemporary information. But Wagner, not knowing of these kinds of materials, was concerned with how the new music school would teach students the styles of earlier music. First, as always, Wagner places the emphasis on performance. First carefully select the music and then, performed in such a fashion that before all else the students in these performances themselves shall have the essence and value of the works disclosed to them by practice in their truest interpretation.[16]

[16] Ibid., 200ff.

Several times he makes this point: where there are questions about early stylistic matter they must be solved by 'practical tests of its effect,' meaning through performance, hearing the music. And again, the goal is to form students 'with the sense and judgment of true and beautiful performance.' He adds in passing that this is the best way to teach music history.

I find it quite interesting that for Wagner the final test, 'should there remain any doubt in the School itself as to the correct method for this or that musical work of a remoter period,' was the public, who 'unbiased by scholastic study and solely guided by the instinctive Feeling would mostly give the right and final verdict.' Here Wagner was speaking from his own experience in being part of the audience, but he was quite correct. Due to the amount of genetic musical material we bring with us at birth, together with the universality of the basic emotions, the audience simply cannot be fooled. Many times I have heard a conductor, introducing a new composition, tell the audience, 'Now this is a really good composition!' And it never has the slightest influence on their opinion.

Wagner's final point in this regard should be always held in mind by the conductor and performer as a very dangerous pitfall. As he points out, artists in other fields, such as Dante, Shakespeare, Calderon, Goethe and the great earlier painters of Italy and the Netherlands had no difficulty in giving their works serious aesthetic qualities. But music, Wagner points out, always has, no matter how serious, 'the purely physical pleasure, the purely sensuous entertainment to be found in her.'[17] This is what makes both programming and the general presentation of a classical concert so tricky. It can so easily step across the line and become an entertainment event.

[17] Ibid., 217.

Well, perhaps the reader will wonder what happened to this plan for the development of a state conservatory? The king appointed a committee, which included Wagner, Hans von Bülow and the composer, Franz Lachner, and others. They submitted a plan which was immediately rejected as too expensive. Two years later a modified version of the school was begun under the directorship of von Bülow, who was soon forced out by anti-Wagner political factions.

It is easy to see, therefore, that Wagner, having come in conflict with political barriers, gave some more thought to the very idea of the State's relationship to education. In one article he points out that the very idea of aesthetic music, music with no object, is incomprehensible to the State which only wants education to produce educated workers.[18] He found the university in Germany in 1867 to be geared to the rich, for people who 'didn't need to learn anything save what they had a fancy for.'

[18] This discussion is found in 'German Art and German Policy,' in ibid., 4:109ff.

> Classical education proper, that is the foundation of all humanizing cul-
> ture upon a knowledge of the Greek and Roman tongues and literature,
> is already openly decried—by persons, too, who as artists make a claim
> to culture—and dubbed both useless and easy of replacement. These
> studies are looked on as a waste of time, disturbing, and good for noth-
> ing but being forgotten.

And with regard to the State and the Arts, Wagner finds a condition which will sound very familiar to the modern reader.

> To want to bring the *State* directly into play for Art, as has already
> occurred to many a well-meaning mind, reposes on an error which takes
> the faults in organization of the modern State for its truest and intrinsic
> essence. The State is the representative of absolute expedience; it knows
> nothing but expedience; and therefore, with the utmost propriety,
> it flatly declines to concern itself with anything that cannot plead a
> directly useful end.[19]

[19] Ibid., 114ff.

Here Wagner cannot help but recall a famous remark by Frederick the Great, 'I want nothing from the State but money and soldiers.'

In an essay written seven years after his study of a State music school for Munich, Wagner had some additional thoughts on the importance of the cultural development of the nation and the responsibility which educational institutions have in creating that culture. The essential matter, Wagner says, is how (Classical) music is viewed by the public.

We find these [educational institutions] have absolutely no influence on the musical taste of the public, save this at most—they send incompetent conductors to our orchestras and above all to our theaters. Forever in the position of the fox to the grapes, regarding Opera, which none of those majestic Conservatories can reach with any measure of success. They play their music by themselves. Their Trios, Quintets, Suites and Psalms are played behind closed doors, so strictly closed as to admit no one but the Messieurs Composers and executants.[20]

[20] 'The German Opera-Stage of Today,' in ibid., 5:279.

Once again, now six years later, in 1878, Wagner is still returning to his original concerns about formal music education. He was still most concerned about authentic tradition in the performance of early music. He recognizes the potential influence which State schools will have on performance practice—but who taught *them*?

I challenge all directors of so-called 'High-schools'—schools, that is, for teaching something more than instrumental technique, or harmony and counterpoint—to say from whom, then, they and their appointed teachers learnt that 'higher' thing which entitles them to give their institute so grand a label? Where is the school that taught themselves? Haply at our theaters and concerts, those privileged establishments for the ruin and maltreatment of our singers, and in particular our orchestra members? Who showed it to them? Tradition, perhaps? But we have not one tradition for such works. Who taught them the interpretation of Mozart and Beethoven, whose works have grown up wild among us, and certainly without the tending of their authors? Why, only eighteen years after Weber's death, and at the very place where for many years he himself had led their performance, I found the tempi of his operas so falsified that nothing but the faithful memory of the master's widow, then still living, could aid my feelings!

I, too, have been to no school for the purpose, but I reaped a negative lesson as to the proper interpretation of our great works of music from my deep and growing disgust at the performances I heard of our great music, whether at High-school concerts or on the military parade.[21]

[21] 'Introduction to Bayreuther Blätter,' in ibid., 6:23ff.

On Musical Grammar

Wagner, in his praise of Beethoven, mentions in passing the famous composer's grammar.

> In long, connected tracts of sound, as in larger, smaller, or even smallest fragments, it turned beneath the Master's poet hand to vowels, syllables and words and phrases of a speech in which a message hitherto unheard, and never spoken yet, could promulgate itself. Each letter of this speech was an infinitely soul-full element.[22]

[22] 'The Art-Work of the Future,' in ibid., 1:121.

Wagner describes the smallest harmony here as 'soul-filled,' but we do not teach harmony this way. You will not hear the harmony teacher use words like 'pain' and 'sorrow.' We only teach it as an abstract language, like a foreign language, where the symbol has a purpose, usually of movement, but has no character. Wagner is quite right when he criticizes us for our superficial understanding of harmony and for our teaching it as something for the eye.

> The eye knows but the surface of this sea; its depth the depth of Heart alone can fathom.[23]

[23] 'The Art-Work of the Future,' in ibid., 1:112.

For Wagner the epitome of teaching compositional technique divorced from Feeling was counterpoint. He says it is not even music, it is the antithesis of music because it is all about technique divorced from emotional meaning. That is important because the purpose of music is to communicate feeling to a listener.

> Counterpoint, with its multiple births and offshoots, is music's artificial playing-with-itself, the mathematics of Feeling, the mechanical rhythm of egoistic Harmony. In its invention, abstract music indulged her whim to pass as the sole and only self-supporting Art. As if it were an art which owes its being, its absolute and godlike nature, to no human Need whatsoever, but purely to *itself*. The willful quite naturally believes itself the absolute and right monopolist and it is certain that to her own caprice alone could Music thank her self-sufficient airs, for that mechanical, contrapuntal artifice was quite incapable of answering any *soul-need*.
>
> Music therefore, in her pride, had become her own direct antithesis: from a heart's concern to a matter of the intellect; from the utterance of unshackled Christian soul's-desire to the cashbook of a modern market-speculation.[24]

[24] 'The Art-Work of the Future,' in ibid., 1:118.

On the Substitution of the Study of Grammar for Score Study

Felix Weingartner, a famous conductor in the generation after Wagner made a thorough study, interviewing musicians who knew the great composer, of Wagner as a conductor. As part of his conclusions, Weingartner addresses the basic bicameral nature of man, the Rational versus Feeling, with respect to the conductor's work: is it the basis of analytical score study or the result of experience and intuitive feeling.

Added to this desire for clarity in Wagner was the passionate temperament with which, aided by a keen understanding, he threw himself into his work; he brought to it also a faculty of immediate communication with the players and imposition of his will on them … *There is no performance of genius possible without temperament.* This truth must be perpetually insisted on … Temperament, however, can be given neither by education, nor conscientiousness, nor, by the way, by favor; it must be *inborn*, the free gift of nature … But [performances of genius] are quite incomprehensible to those 'aesthetes' who consider them as problems of the understanding and would solve them, like a mathematical problem, by analysis.[25]

During 1850 Wagner began to be more than usually frustrated with criticism, in particular because he was now becoming aware of criticism by people who proclaimed to be his friends. His response came in a tract called, 'A Communication to my Friends,' in which his basic message was 'take all of me or none of me.' In his efforts to describe his frustration, Wagner makes some very important comments of a universal nature. Thinking of the way literary critics analyze his music only on the basis of grammar (harmony, etc.), he says that to attempt to separate the Artist from the Man is 'as brainless an attempt as the divorce of soul and body.'[26] The music of an artist such as himself can not be understood unless that understanding is also grounded in sympathy, 'upon the fellow-pain and fellow-feeling with the veriest human aspect of his life.'

Wagner is absolutely correct when he raises this question: Can one really understand music only on the basis of academic, objective analysis of the grammar of the music, or is it necessary to have a deeper understanding of human nature in order

[25] Felix Weingartner, *On Conducting* (New York: Kalmus, 1906), 10ff.

[26] This tract is found in 'A Communication to my Friends,' in Wagner, *Richard Wagner's Prose Works*, 269ff.

to truly understand the communication of universal Truth found in a fine composition? We do not teach this distinction to young conductors.

It is easy to understand the educator's defense, 'the young person lacks sufficient experience to perceive universal human Truths in music.' Strictly speaking that may not be true, for as we learn more about the genetic aspects of both music and the emotions which accompany us at birth it may well be that the student is more prepared for universality than we presently think. But, I will let that pass for the moment and grant the educator's point. But the real mistake of the teacher of musical grammar is his failure to overlook one of the most fundamental foundations of knowledge and to mislead his students by not making it very clear that everything on paper is *only a symbol of something else*. That something else is the real music and that is what was of concern to Wagner. Instead, in school we teach the grammar of music as if it *were* the music and we lead young conductors to think that by drawing Roman numerals under chords they are analyzing the music. Nothing could be further from the truth. An example: I was once requested by the Library of Congress to review a specific dissertation, a DMA study by a young conductor, for one of their publications. The dissertation purported to analyze a composition by Karel Husa from two perspectives, an analysis of the music and the identification of conducting problems. There was a passage where the composer, in communication with the student, had mentioned that this portion of the music was written just after learning of the death of his father and thus reflected his pain and sorrow. The student, in writing of this passage, found as the 'challenges for the conductor' such things as very little time to get a mute in, or a difficult high note on some woodwind instrument, etc. But nothing was said of the most important challenge for the conductor, how to communicate the composer's pain and sorrow.

This student, like most music students, arrive at the doctoral level without ever being told that the things we see on paper are not music, they are only symbols, an agreed upon language to represent the real thing. And yet, Aristotle made this point so clear two thousand five hundred years ago. He reminded his students that, to give an example, when we write 'c–a–t' it is only an agreed upon means of putting on paper a representative symbol, of what we mean when we *say* 'cat.' But, he continued, when we *say* 'cat' it is *also* only a symbol of the real thing. Therefore written language is two generations removed from the real thing. And so it is in music notation. And let us not forget, musicians prospered and successfully communicated to listeners for perhaps a million years before anything was ever written on paper!

But we teach only the symbols, the grammar of music, and not music. Wagner says we teach only the 'ghost of art.' How then do we teach the student to find the music in a score? First, and foremost, we must teach the student to learn to identify the emotions and feeling in the music, for the only true purpose of music is to communicate emotion. But as Wagner points out, the intellect alone will not take the student there,

> But … this understanding cannot be compassed by the sheer unaided pure Intellect, but only by the Feeling.[27]

But going further, through identifying with the emotion of a score the conductor must so sympathize with the composer that he adopts 'the aim as his very own and takes on an intimate and weighty share (with the composer) in its realization.'

From Wagner's perspective, the second error in our pedagogy is that by teaching the conductor to base his artistic discoveries in a score upon the basis of his identifying the formal hallmarks of music theory—identifying chords, forms, etc.,—we are teaching the student to value himself according to the past tense *outer* world instead of the teacher finding ways to relate music to the student's own present tense *inner* world.

> If I seek to gain myself a fairly satisfactory explanation of the artistic faculty, I can only do so by attributing it chiefly to the force of the receptive faculty. The un-artistic academic[28] temperament may be characterized thus: that from youth up it sets a check upon impressions from the outside, which, in the course of the man's development, mounts even to a calculation of the personal profit that his withstanding of the outer world will bring him, to a talent for referring this outer world to himself and never himself to it. On the other hand, the artistic temperament is marked by this one feature: that its owner gives himself up without reserve to the impressions which move his emotional being to sympathy.[29]

[27] This tract is found in 'A Communication to my Friends,' in ibid., 269ff.

[28] Since Wagner associated education with the state he used the word 'political' where I use 'academic.'

[29] 'A Commnication to my Friends,' in Wagner, *Richard Wagner's Prose Works*, 286.

In addition, of course, the traditional system of enforcing general rules as the standard ignores another fundamental foundation of art, one very important to Wagner.

> Until we come to recognize, and on every hand to demonstrate in practice, that the very essence of the human species consists in the diversity of human individuality …[30]

[30] 'A Commnication to my Friends,' in ibid., 276. Wagner adds that both State and Church were guilty of suppressing the individual.

All these elements of grammar which the academic sets before the student are by their very nature rational data and it is physically impossible for them to contribute to the real educational goal of music—the communication of emotion. Nothing puts this in clearer focus than some notes Wagner left, notes made for himself and not for publication, which are the result and sum of his personal analysis of the C-sharp Minor Quartet of Beethoven. Here was his 1855 analysis,

> [*Adagio*] Melancholy morning prayer of a deeply suffering heart.
> [*Allegro*] Graceful apparition, rousing fresh desire of life.
> [*Andante and variations*] Charm, sweetness, longing, love
> [*Scherzo*] Whim, humor, high spirits.
> [*Finale*] Passing over to resignation. Most sorrowful renunciation.

In summary, Wagner believed the teacher has the duty to communicate to the student two fundamental things about a score. These are the identification of the emotional elements and the means and success (or not) by which the composer communicates these through his notation.

> Whosoever feels impelled, then, to bear witness to his lack of understanding of an artwork should take the precaution to ask himself one simple question, namely: what were the reasons for this lack? True, that he would come back at last to the qualities of the artwork itself, but only after he had cleared up the immediate problem of the physical appearance in which it had addressed itself to his feelings. Was this outward appearance unable to arouse or pacify his feelings, then he would have, before all else, to endeavor to procure himself an insight into a manifest imperfection of the artwork; namely, into the grounds of a failure of correspondence between the purpose of the artist and the nature of those means by which he sought to impart it to the hearer's Feeling. Only two issues could then lie open for his inquiry, namely: whether the means of presentation to the senses were in keeping with the artistic aim, or whether this aim itself was indeed an artistic one?[31]

[31] 'A Commnication to my Friends,' in ibid., 1:271.

In what course in the university today do we teach the student to contemplate on either of these?

Wagner on the Ethics of Conducting

> Berlioz ... does not compose for gold ...
> [Thus] the rest of the Parisian world avoids him as a madman.[1]

> Popularity, the curse of every grand and noble thing.[2]

The two above quotations from Wagner might seem to the reader of today's world to represent a very narrow view. But in fact the views expressed in these two quotations mirror the advice of the greatest thinkers of the past two thousand years as they explained to the young artists of their generations the basic choice before them: to be an artist that expresses the deepest feeling within your self, or to amuse the public. No early philosopher, from Aristotle forward, ever thought there was a middle ground.

These two quotations also epitomize what Wagner heard from theater managers and court officials every day during his frustrating early years when he was trying to get performances of his early operas. During his years of political exile, when he could not return to Germany and lived in Switzerland, he had time to give extended thought to many areas of art, including the subject at hand, the relationship of the artist and the public.

To begin with the composer, it was very clear to Wagner that aesthetic music of the highest value can only come from the feelings inside the composer and not for any outer purpose.

> Everything lives and lasts by the inner Necessity of its being, by its own nature's Need. It lay in the nature of the art of music to evolve herself to a capability of the most definite and manifold expression [of that which] lay hid within her soul.[3]

He composes abstracted from outer things, with what earlier writers called 'divine fury.' Only when he is finished does he think about the outer world, including his hopes for a good reception of his work by the public. But as the true artist's thoughts return to the driving inner inspiration which helped him create the music the outer world loses its power over him.

[1] Wagner, an autobiographical sketch (1842) found in Richard Wagner, *Richard Wagner's Prose Works*, trans. William Ashton Ellis (New York: Broude Brothers, 1966), 1:15.

[2] 'A Happy Evening,' in ibid., 7:75.

[3] 'Opera and the Nature of Music,' part 1, in ibid., 2:35.

The naïve, truly inspired artist casts himself with reckless enthusiasm into his artwork and only when it is finished, when it shows itself in all its actuality, does he win from practical experience that genuine force of Reflection which preserves him in general from illusions, yet in the specific case of his feeling driven again to his composition by his inspiration, loses once more its power over him completely.[4]

Let me pause here briefly to put this in a modern context. Suppose there were a composition called 'George Washington Bridge.' What Wagner is trying to make clear is that such a composition has nothing whatsoever to do with the description of a bridge. Rather the composition has to do with the composer's own, personal feelings when he thinks about or sees the bridge. The composition, once again, is about him, not the bridge. It follows, as Wagner tries to explain in the immediately previous quotation, that the fine aesthetic composer really writes for himself and not the public. I once heard someone say that when Beethoven died he would have been perfectly content to have all his scores gathered up and have them buried with him in the ground. I believe that is true.

To return to Wagner, he begins to focus his thoughts by taking the reader on a little Reality Tour, which he begins with Mozart who was so richly talented that he could just sit down and compose without any cares of the public or the market.

There is nothing more characteristic of Mozart in his career as an opera composer than the unconcernedness with which he went to work. It was so far from occurring to him to weigh the pros and cons of the aesthetic problem involved in opera that he rather engaged with utmost unconstraint in setting any and every operatic libretto offered him, almost heedless whether it were a thankful or a thankless task for him as a pure musician …

He was so utterly and entirely a musician, and nothing but musician …[5]

…

How little did Mozart, this richest gifted of all musicians, understand our modern composers trick of building gaudy towers of music upon a hollow, a valueless foundation.[6]

4 'Opera and the Nature of Music,' part 1, in ibid., 2:36.

5 Ibid. 'An End in Paris,' is found in ibid., 7:46ff.

6 Ibid., 2:37.

At the other extreme Wagner places Rossini, a man also richly talented but who chose to compose for money and the good life it brings. Wagner coins a perfectly marvelous phrase to characterize Rossini's music: 'Rossini's melodies are like artificial flowers, made of silk.'[7]

7 Ibid., 2:41.

8 Ibid., 2:42.

To live was what Rossini intended. To do this he saw well enough that he must live with those who had ears to hear him. The only living thing he had come upon in opera was absolute melody, so he merely needed to pay heed to the kind of melody he must strike in order to be heard. He turned his back on the pedantic lumber of heavy scores and listened where the people sang without a written note. What he heard there was what, out of all the operatic box of tricks, had stayed the most unbidden in the ear: the *naked, ear-delighting, absolute-melodic Melody*, i.e., melody that was just melody and nothing else, that glides into the ear—one knows not why; that one picks up—one knows not why; that one exchanges today with that of yesterday, and forgets again tomorrow—also, one knows not why; that sounds sad when we are merry and merry when we are out of sorts; and that still we hum to ourselves and we haven't a ghost of knowledge why.[8]

In Wagner's view Rossini killed opera as a serious dramatic form. Once it became an entertainment vehicle driven by Rossini's engaging melodies, the character of singing, the quality of the orchestral performance and even the literary value of the libretto no longer mattered. 'He made the Public, with all its whims and wishes, the determinative factor in Opera.'[9]

9 Ibid., 2:44.

Wagner associates Beethoven with Columbus, for he started out to do merely one thing and ended up discovering something else, a new world.

10 Ibid., 2:71ff.

For us, too, has there been unveiled the exhaustless power of Music, through Beethoven's all-puissant error. Through his undaunted toil to reach the artistically Necessary within an artistically Impossible is shown us Music's restricted faculty of accomplishing every thinkable task, if only she consent to stay what she really is—an *art of Expression*.[10]

In Wagner's view, as long as Beethoven stayed within the expectations of the common style (in his early period) he had wide appreciation. But later 'there awoke in the artist a longing for distinct expression of specific, characteristically individual emotions.' Now the 'agony of this deep-stirred man' was no longer understood by the broad audience.

Upon the curious hearer who did not understand him, simply because the inspired man could not possibly make himself intelligible to such an one, these mighty transports and the half-sorrowful, half-blissful stammerings of a Pythian inspiration, could not but make the impression of a genius stricken with madness.[11]

[11] Ibid., 2:72

The immediate followers of Beethoven, Wagner found, not being able to match the deep 'unspoken secret of the master' tried to imitate the external forms by writing programmatic works and symphonies with vocal parts. However most following German composers took a more conservative, safe route. Do you know composers today who fall into the following description by Wagner?

They sought to save themselves from the consequences of that expressional manner by polishing down its most jutting angles and by taking up again the older fashions of expression … They formed themselves an artificial mixture that we can only call a general Abstract style of music, in which one might go on composing with great propriety and respectability for quite a length of time without much fear of its being seriously disturbed by drastic individualities. If Beethoven mostly gives us the impression of a man who has something to tell us, which yet he cannot plainly impart, on the other hand these modern followers of his appear like men who, often in a charmingly circumstantial fashion, impart to us the news that they have nothing at all to say.[12]

[12] Ibid., 2:74

We have to forgive Wagner for his harsh criticism of another very famous composer during his life time, Meyerbeer, for this man could have helped Wagner in his period of need and on the contrary worked against him.

In Meyerbeer's music there is shown so appalling an emptiness, shallowness and artistic nothingness that … we are tempted to set down his specific musical capacity at zero.[13]

[13] Ibid., 2:100.

Nevertheless, Wagner's own sense of ethics and fair play forced him to admit that there are places in the music of Meyerbeer where he achieves momentary greatness.

… so soon as he treads the soil of a Necessity stronger than his self-seeking Caprice; of a necessity which suddenly guides his erring footsteps, to his own salvation and into the paths of sterling Art.[14]

[14] Ibid., 2:101

Wagner now pauses to reflect on his own place in the Reality Tour. In 1848 a series of revolutions shook France, Germany, Austria, and Italy and eventually spread to Latin America. The period was sometimes called 'Springtime of the Peoples,' because it was fueled in part by a demand for more democracy. The economic disruptions leading to these revolutions made life even more difficult for Wagner while living in Paris attempting to gain productions of his early operas. Indeed, out of financial necessity, he was forced to spend the winter of 1840–1841 arranging opera arias for various instruments, including for cornet.

If the reader can imagine Wagner at this time, full of confidence in his own talent and yet living in real poverty and having met with no success with the establishment in producing his *Rienzi*, you will understand his fundamental frustration with society. No doubt for the purpose of gaining a little money, he wrote a little fictional newspaper story called 'An End in Paris.' The story is of interest because it is obviously an autobiographical reference to his own rejection in Paris. It is the story of a poor young German who has gathered together his last funds in order to travel to Paris,

> the center of the world, where the arts of every nation stream together to one focus; where the artists of each race find recognition; and where I hope for satisfaction of the tiny morsel of ambition that Heaven— apparently in inadvertence—has set in my own breast.

The young artist came to Paris promising himself that in one year he would become renown. Later, in recounting his failure, he recalls it was not due to some dramatic storm, such as which sinks ships, but rather he was brought to financial ruin by 'quagmires and swamps, in which I sank.'

These quagmires and swamps were, he explained, the ante-chambers of palaces and official government buildings where he spent his year sitting, waiting to present himself for employment and to be interviewed by some functionary. 'Into the Ante-chambers of Hunger I fell!'

> In those Ante-chambers I dreamed away a fair year of my life. I dreamt of many wondrous mad and fabled stories from the 'Thousand and One Nights,' of men and beasts, of gold and offal. My dreams were of gods and contrabassists, of jeweled snuffboxes and prima-donnas, of satin

gowns and lovesick lords, of chorus-girls and five-franc pieces. Between
I sometimes seemed to hear the wailing, ghost-like note of an oboe;
that note thrilled through my every nerve and cut into my heart. One
day when I had dreamed my maddest, and that oboe note was tingling
through me at its sharpest, I suddenly awoke and found I had become
a madman.

He is convinced he is to die and he climbs the summit of
Montmartre, an area of Paris traditionally the home of poor
artists, where he rents a room and sends someone to gather his
scores and papers,

which I had stowed in a wretched hovel in the city; for, alas! I had never
succeeded in pawning them. So here I lie, determined to pass away in
God and pure Music.

He begs a friend to pay his debts, arrange for his funeral and to
hear his final will and testament,

I believe in God, Mozart and Beethoven and likewise their disciples
and apostles.
    I believe in the Holy Spirit and the truth of the one, indivisible Art;
I believe that this Art proceeds from God and lives within the hearts of
all illumined men; I believe that he who once has bathed in the sublime
delights of this high Art is consecrate to Her forever and never can
deny Her.
    I believe that through this Art all men are saved and therefore each
may die for Her of hunger.
    I believe that on earth I was a jarring discord, which will at once be
perfectly resolved by death.
    I believe in a last judgment which will condemn to fearful pains all
those who in this world have dared to play the huckster with chaste Art
and have violated and dishonored Her through evilness of heart and
ribald lust of senses. I believe that these will be condemned through all
eternity to hear their own vile music.

After the death of this neglected artist, the narrator wonders
at the cost of his death to society.

Who knows what died in this child of man, leaving no trace behind?
Was it a Mozart, or a Beethoven? Who can tell, and who can gainsay me
when I claim that in him there fell an artist who would have enriched
the world with his creations, had he not been forced to die too soon
of hunger?[15]

[15] The story is found in ibid., 7:46ff.

WAGNER ON THE ETHICS OF CONDUCTING   35

It was during this revolutionary period in Paris that Wagner began to contemplate at length on the nature of art and society, the result of which would become his important essay, 'Art and Revolution.' He began to think of the effects of the revolution, with respect to its contribution toward freeing the people from the yoke of the aristocracy, as a symbol of his ideal of Art being freed from the conditions of its existence.[16] He believed Art to be the highest form of freedom and in his 'Art and Revolution' he gives the reader a brief history of the struggles of Art against various obstacles set before it by society, such as the Romans' preference for Entertainment, the prohibitions by the Roman Church and the wars and poverty of the Middle Ages.[17]

Through this long struggle, from ancient Greece to the nineteenth century, Music prevailed only to lose its way and now, 'preferred to sell her soul and body to a far worse mistress—*Commerce.*' From the perspective of a pure artist like Wagner, this turn in the goal of musicians had most disconcerting results.

> This the Art, as it now fills the entire civilized world! Its true essence is Industry; its ethical aim, the gaining of gold; its aesthetic purpose, the entertainment of those whose time hangs heavily on their hands. From the heart of our modern society, from the golden calf of whole-sale Speculation, stalled at the meeting of its cross-roads, our art sucks forth its life-juice, borrows a hollow grave from the lifeless relics of the chivalric conventions of medieval times, and—blushing not to fleece the poor, for all its professions of Christianity—descends to the depths of the proletariat, enervating, demoralizing and dehumanizing everything on which it sheds its venom.

At the heart of this decline in the most noble goals of our musical art Wagner finds first and foremost a tendency of the artist to follow the lure of the applause of the world of entertainment. Now, he finds, even opera is being proclaimed as a form of entertainment and, with even more drastic results, the threat follows in the warning that if one does not make his art popular he will lose the public's support. Does this sound familiar to the reader?

[16] 'An Introduction to Art and Revolution,' in ibid., 1:29.

[17] This discussion is found under 'Art and Revolution,' in ibid., 1:35ff.

There are even many of our most popular artists who do not in the least conceal the fact that they have no other ambition than to satisfy this shallow audience. They are wise in their generation; for when the prince leaves a heavy dinner, the banker a fatiguing financial operation, the working man a weary day of toil, and go to the theater, they ask for rest, distraction and amusement and are in no mood for renewed effort and fresh expenditure of force … We shall then be told that if we do not employ Art in this manner, it must perish from out our public life: i.e., that the artist will lose the means of living.

Not only must true aesthetic music have the strength of character to set itself above the lures of gold and the empty applause of entertainment, but Wagner warns of one additional distraction, 'that thing is *Fame*!'

Yet what sort of fame is there to reach in our public art? Only the fame of the same publicity for which this art is planned, and which the fame-lusting man can never obtain but by submission to its most trivial claims. Thus he deludes both himself and the public, in giving it his piebald art-work; while the public deludes both itself and him, in bestowing on him its applause. But this mutual lie is worthy of the lying nature of modern Fame itself.

For a time Wagner thought perhaps the best means of preserving the most lofty goals of our art would lie in some form of government supervision. To this end, during the years 1848–1849 when much of Europe was caught up in the reorganizing of civil affairs, Wagner was inspired to write a paper on the goals of reorganizing the State theaters into a single unified structure. He provides the overriding goal in a single sentence:

The Theater should have no other purpose, than to work for the ennobling of taste and manners.[18]

[18] 'A National Theatre,' in ibid., 7:324.

In a similar vein he wanted to create unions for the playwrights and composers for the protection and promotion of their work and their task Wagner defined as,

to watch over the preservation of the *aesthetic*, *ethical* and *national* purity of the National theater.

His urgency for these goals came from his disappointing experience when he was employed in the theater in Dresden. The presumption of the theater management was that the theater was needed because the city had many visitors who wouldn't know what to do with themselves in the evening otherwise.

> In our opinion this [requires] the bitterest condemnation of the prevailing estimate of the Theatre. So, only when people don't know what to do with a tiresome evening, will they go to the theatre? In effect, with a large section of the public this view has become a habit, and the Theatre accordingly has sunk to a mere source of entertainment, a pastime as surrogate for playing cards and so forth.
>
> If we did not start with a far higher and worthier opinion of the Theatre, and seek to bring it to common acceptance, we fail to see by what right we could ever demand the active support of the nation for this institute. Our view is a nobler one; we claim the fullest and keenest interest of the whole nation for an artistic establishment that combines all the arts with the object of ennobling taste and manners.

Wagner stressed this last point at some length[19] and suggested that the experience of the period of Beethoven's music changed the character of the average German in the following years.

[19] Ibid., 7:355.

Nothing came of his plan for a national theater to preserve the *aesthetic*, *ethical* and *national* purity, so at length he realized that it is in the individual artist that this battle between art and commerce must be won. But he now gives the artist an additional burden, the maintenance of the national spirit. This he addresses in an article called 'What is German?' Here he gives credit to Bach and Goethe for first announcing to the world the essence of the German spirit.[20] Wagner states his understanding of this in the form of a motto ready to be etched in bronze.

[20] This discussion can be found in 'What is German?' in ibid., 4:162ff.

The Beautiful and Noble came not into the world for sake of profit, nay, not for sake of even fame and recognition.

For Wagner the personification of this German spirit was Bach. He paints the most pathetic picture of the great man, 'insanely muffled in the French full-bottomed wig … slinking from one Thuringian parish to another, puny places scarcely known to us by name.' It took an entire century, Wagner reminds us, to drag his works from oblivion yet 'it is impossible to denote its wealth, its sublimity, its all-embracing import, through any manner of comparison.' And while Bach was buried without notice or ceremony, at the same time,

> the large and little Courts of German princes were swarming with Italian opera-composers and virtuosi, brought with untold outlay, too, to shower on slighted Germany the leavings of an art that nowadays cannot be accorded the least consideration.

Retaining his concentration on the individual artist, in an article called 'The Virtuoso and the Artist,' Wagner concentrates on the question of what the composer expects from the performer. He makes it clear that it is not what he wrote on paper that he wishes to be communicated, but 'the thoughts of his *spirit* may be transmitted unalloyed and undisfigured to the organs of perception.'[21] For this purpose he recommends it is best if a composer conducts his own work.

[21] This article is found in ibid., 7:108ff.

If the composer is not available for conducting, then the next best alternative is another composer, or one sufficiently endowed with creative power to understand the composer's intent and be able to offer him 'a certain loving pliability.' The next best alternative would be conductors with no claim as composers but who are modest enough to 'so entirely sink their personal attributes that neither their defects nor their advantages should come to light in the performance.'

First and foremost the composer does not welcome the 'distracting individuality of the performer.' The most to be feared is that type of virtuoso who 'here runs, there jumps; he melts, he pines, he paws and glides, and the audience is fettered to his fingers.' Such a virtuoso creates a mood where your composition 'does not warm, but glitters.' But Wagner admits there are some virtuosi who are different, great artists who owe their reputation to their moving execution of the noblest compositions of the greatest masters.

Here Wagner returns to a constant concern: programming which mixes serious aesthetic compositions with popular music. You see the advertisement and 'one name shines on you: *Beethoven*! Enough!' That name alone is reason to attend the concert.

WAGNER ON THE ETHICS OF CONDUCTING 39

Here is the concert hall. And positively, Beethoven appears to you [but] all around sit high-bred ladies, row after row of high-bred ladies and in a wide half-moon behind them lively gentlemen with lorgnettes in the eye. But Beethoven is there, midst all the perfumed agony of dream-rocked elegance. It really is Beethoven, sinewed and broad, in all his sad omnipotence. But, who comes there with him?

Great God! Guillaume Tell, Robert the Devil, and—who after these? Weber, the tender and true! Good! And then, a Galop! O heavens! Who-ever has once written gallops himself, who has had his stir in Potpour-ris, knows what a want can drive us to when it is a question of drawing near to Beethoven at all costs. I took the measure of the awful need that could drive another man today to Pot-pourris and Galops, to gain the chance of preaching Beethoven; and though I must admire the virtuoso in this instance, I cursed all virtuosity.[22]

Returning to the subject of who should interpret a composer's music, Wagner now gives us a portrait of the one artist he neglected to mention in the foregoing discussion, the conductor.

Lo there the man who certainly thinks least about himself, and to whom the personal act of pleasing has surely nothing special to bring in, the man beating time for an orchestra. He surely fancies he has bored to the very inside of the composer, ay, has drawn him on like a second skin? You won't tell me that *he* is plagued with the Upstart-devil, when he takes your tempo wrong, misunderstands your expression marks and drives you to desperation at listening to your own composition. Yet he can be a virtuoso too, and tempt the public by all kinds of spicy nuances into thinking that it after all is he who makes the whole thing sound so nice. He finds it neat to let a loud passage be played quite soft, for a change, a fast one a wee bit slower; he will add you, here and there, a trombone effect, or a dash of the cymbals and triangle; but his chief resource is a drastic cut, if he otherwise is not quite sure of his success.[23] Him we must call a virtuoso of the Baton.

But Wagner realized that the conductor was just as susceptible to the lures of entertainment as any other artist. Indeed, he confesses that in his youth he himself fell victim to this attraction

I recall to mind a readiness to warm myself at any of that artworld's foolishness which showed the least resemblance to my goal: their sickly unsubstantiality was mantled with a glittering show, such as never had I seen before. It was only later, that I became conscious how greatly I deceived myself in this respect, through an almost artificial state of nervous excitation. This gratuitous excitement, mounting glibly to the

[22] These kinds of concerts of very mixed repertoire were common in the nineteenth century and the translator infers that this passage was inspired by a recital in 1840 during which Liszt performed a program which included an arrangement of a Beethoven symphony for piano, various transcriptions of arias and songs and concluding with a Galop Chromatique. The translator suggests that Liszt's fantasia on Robert le diable was probably played as an encore. These very 'popular' looking programs were common during the first half of the nineteenth century. Hummel, for example, arranged the first seven Beethoven symphonies for flute, violin, cello and piano.

[23] When a student at the University of Michigan I performed under a staff conductor, who, having elected to perform a transcription of the first movement of the Franck D minor Symphony, thought it best to leave out the development section to insure against boredom on the part of the audience.

verge of transport, was nourished all unawares to myself by the feeling of my outward lot; which I must have recognized as completely hopeless, if I had suddenly acknowledged to myself that all this artistic tinsel that made up the world in which I was striving to press forward was inwardly an object of my deepest loathing.[24]

But, he warns, boredom is rarely cured by entertainment music.

> The places in our halls of entertainment are mostly filled by nothing but that section of our citizen society whose only ground for change of occupation is utter boredom. The disease of boredom, however, is not remediable by sips of Art, for it can never be distracted of set purpose but merely duped into another form of boredom.[25]

Regarding popular outdoors concerts, Wagner, in his 'A Happy Evening,' comments that he has never understood why some people 'found any pleasure in *seeing* music, instead of hearing it.'[26]

This discussion leads to repertoire, another vital ethical concern, for as Wagner points out the repertoire selection is where the 'public and artist fit each other.'[27] In 1878 he became interested in Time and Space and produced an article for the *Bayreuther Blätter* in October of that year. He points to important people who were ahead of their times and misunderstood by their contemporaries, including Plato, Calderon, Dante and the Renaissance philosopher, Giordano Bruno, who was burned at the stake 'by the stupid monks,' yet would have been worshiped as a holy man had he but lived on the Ganges. An even more ancient example he provides are the ancient Greek tragedies.

> If we are obliged to get Time and Place, with their manners … explained to us by scholars who often know nothing at all of the subject, we may be sure we have forever lost the clue to something that once came to light in another age and country.

It is to honor the original integrity of a work such as Mozart's *Marriage of Figaro* that Wagner strongly opposes the translation into other languages. A work such as Mozart's *Magic Flute*, while intended for a specific audience in a specific city, yet 'stands solitary and assignable to no age whatsoever' due to its remarkable quality. Yet he wonders if perhaps we

[24] 'A Communication to my Friends,' in Wagner, *Richard Wagner's Prose Works*, 1:302.

[25] 'Judaism in Music,' in ibid., 3:96ff.

[26] 'A Happy Evening,' in ibid., 7:70.

[27] 'The Public in Time and Space,' in ibid., 6:85ff.

cannot really understand this work unless we were magically transported back in time to the Theater an der Wien and the year of its first production. Could you really appreciate this work, for example, in a court performance in modern Berlin?

Wagner seems to have been thinking here of the difficulty of programming works such as the Tone Poems of Liszt which are based on older historical figures. The question is, can the audience really transport itself back to a different time in order to understand the music? Probably not, for even in a work such as Strauss' *Also sprach Zarathustra*, one of the most frequently performed late nineteenth century compositions, no listener ever thinks about Nietzsche's story upon which it is based.

And then it seems clear that another basic question on Wagner's mind was, Do you program a work that is ahead of the public's experience to understand it? My answer to this is Yes, but only if you are convinced of the aesthetic value of the composition and do not do it just because it is 'interesting' or new, etc.

Wagner raises several other ethical considerations relevant to repertoire in a newspaper article of 1879, 'On Poetry and Composition.'[28] Wagner was first disturbed by the growing influence of newspaper critics on the public. One of the movements which Wagner attributed to the newspaper men was the idea that a composition must have 'wit,' or some intellectual left hemisphere characteristic in order to be interesting. Music, in other words, can no longer be just music. Wagner responded,

> Music is the most witless thing conceivable … Herr Paul Lindau in particular, who only asks amusement from all Art, as I am told, since otherwise it bores him.
>
> But strange to say, it is precisely our amusing music that is the greatest bore of all (just think of a piece entitled a 'Divertissement' at any of our concerts), whereas—say what you will—a completely witless Symphony of Beethoven's is always too brief for every hearer.

Wagner believed in addition that 'Music indeed has nothing to do with the common seriousness of life.' On the contrary its character is sublime and has grief-assuaging radiance—it

28 This article can be found in ibid., 6:133ff.

smiles on us, but never makes us laugh. A work such as the *A major Symphony* of Beethoven is not merely a 'happy' composition, it is a work of the 'loftiest transport.'

Neither, Wagner warns, must we be misled by a composer's comments about why he wrote a composition. The real key is what inspired the music and frequently the composer cannot put this into words—the whole value of music being that it communicates things you cannot put into words. He gives the example of Hummel.

> The suave, but somewhat philistine *Hummel* once was asked what lovely landscape he had thought of when composing a certain charming Rondo. To tell the simple truth, he might have answered a beautiful fugal theme of Bach's C-sharp major, only he was still more candid and confessed that the eighty ducats of his publisher had swum before his eyes.

The real joke here, says Wagner, is not in the music, but in the composer's pretence of having written finely with the resulting quid-pro-quos. And he adds another example in Mendelssohn who could not find the inspiration for his *Antigone* which he found for his *Hebrides Overture*, which Wagner confesses 'is one of the most beautiful musical works that we possess.'[29]

After presenting all these varieties of ethical decisions facing the performer or conductor, Wagner saves the most import for last. On one hand, clearly music makes no sense without a listener. I go further and say music does not even exist except in live performance and with a listener. Although the audience is therefore a critical factor, Wagner found this a difficult topic.

> The passion for publicity is hard to comprehend.
> Each experience teaches that it is in an evil sphere.[30]

Wagner follows this statement with an unusually bitter reflection on the fate of the composer,

> Here reads the rule: the Public wills to be amused, and thou must seek to smuggle in thine Own beneath the mantle of Amusement.

[29] Brahms once sent a note to Mendelssohn saying he would willingly give up everything he had written to be the composer of the *Hebrides Overture*.

[30] 'The Artist and Publicity,' in ibid., 7:136.

Here he is thinking of all the 'plots and artifices' composers must go through for most of their life to bring before 'the ears of the crowd what it can never understand!' He is sad when he reflects on the past when a composer only had to connect the 'secret history of their heart' with a magic chain that connects with sympathetic souls throughout the centuries, while today there is only 'talk of schools and manners.'

In his 'A Happy Evening,' Wagner suggests that the Beethoven symphonies were composed just for themselves and not for the public at all.[31] He continues this line of thought by saying the reverse is true, the composer should not be influenced by the world around him.

> It would be to drag the musician from his high estate if one tried to make him fit his inspiration to the semblance of that daily world; and still more would that instrumental composer disown his mission, or expose his weakness, who should aim at carrying the cramped proportions of purely worldly things into the province of his art.

In April 1878, Wagner began a series of articles on the ethics of music-making with respect to the public and the general idea of popularity. He begins with a wonderful Indian proverb which he found:

> Bad music is not the worst, for seldom can it deceive;
> Mediocre music is far worse, as many believe it to be good.[32]

Wagner finds many curious Truths on this subject, as for example, 'Everything, except the good, has its Public.'

> Never do we find an exploiter of the mediocre referring to his confederates, but always to the 'public.'

Being a very well-read man, he follows this by advice offered over thousands of years by various philosophers:

> Without pretending to set up a general principle valid for all epochs and culture, I simply take in eye our public art conductions of the day when I assert that it is impossible for anything to be truly good if it is reckoned in advance for presentation to the public and this intended presentation rules the author in his sketch and composition of an artwork.

[31] Ibid., 7:74.

[32] This can be found in 'Public and Popularity,' in ibid., 6:53.

Wagner's larger concern lay in the fact that he found on concert stages generally that most of the repertoire was mediocre and that the performers themselves, so used to the mediocre, no longer recognized the good. Therefore he doubts that anyone would disagree with his conclusion that in Germany the mediocre is performed very well, by virtue of experience, and the good is performed badly.

> What then is the character of the Mediocre? By this term we commonly signify that which brings us no new and unknown thing, but the known-already in a pleasing and insinuating form. In a good sense, it would be the product of Talent—if we agree with Schopenhauer that Talent hits a mark we all can see, but cannot easily reach; whilst Genius, the genius of 'the Good,' attains a goal we others do not even see.

Wagner finds it necessary here to comment on virtuosity, then a popular occurrence on the German stage. Since the works of the great composers are always available, the man who can play these correctly, 'and in the master's spirit,' can be said to have talent.

> To let his virtuosity sparkle solely for itself, the musician often trumps up pieces of his own, works which belong to the class of the mediocre. In these cases the actual virtuosity cannot in itself be ranked mediocre, but we must candidly confess that a mediocre virtuoso is of no class at all.

In the second article on his series on the public and popularity Wagner considers the nature of the audience in more detail. He praises Paris which has theaters and repertoire designed for specific classes of people. In Germany, however, lacking this planning, one finds such a variety of people in the hall that some understand the work and some do not. He begins with a rather dismal view of the audience in general.

> A large proportion of the audience has fallen on the theater tonight in error and from false supposition. What brought them here may certainly be gauged as nothing but the quest of entertainment, and that in the case of every comer; only, the strange diversity of receptiveness, in kind as in degree, is plainer to the physiognomical observer of a theater public than anywhere else—even than at church, since there hypocrisy conceals what here dares figure unabashed.

Nor are the various grades of society and education to which the spectators belong, by any means an index to the individual's receptiveness. In the most expensive seats, as in the cheapest, one meets the same phenomenon of interest and apathy packed side by side. At one of the excellent first performances of *Tristan* in Munich I observed a vigorous dame of middle age in the last extremity of boredom during the third act, while the cheeks of her husband, a grey-beard superior officer, were streaming with tears of the deepest emotion.[33]

Wagner finds the great variety of repertoire heard on the German stage to be confusing to the audience, with respect to developing their expectations.[34] In addition, reflecting his own history, he believed that the German audience was prejudiced by the critics. Although he regarded them as innocent enough that if one only provides them with the 'true element of soul' it will overcome the advance comments by the critics.[35]

He found that playwrights 'count on and exploit in favor of the Bad.' He cites a phrase used by playwrights, *mundus vult decipi* ['the world wishes to be deceived,' which his friend Liszt 'once playfully turned into *mundus vult Schundus* ['the world wants garbage'].

But what is one to do who is not interested in duping the audience? Probably, says Wagner, better to forget them altogether and devote himself entirely to his own work, 'as from the depths of his own soul.'

Finally, he decides to define the good and the bad. The good, 'exactly like the *Morally good*, springs from no intention, no concern.' By this he refers to the classical definition of high art, that it has no purpose. 'On the contrary, we might define the *Bad* as the sheer aim-to-please.'[36]

Wagner returns to this subject of inferior music in a return to a spurious composer whom he had first presented in an earlier 'An End in Paris.' These little stories are autobiographical and we can measure the guilt Wagner felt in his days of poverty when he was forced to write various popular contributions for a Paris publisher. In the present instance, this unknown German composer has made a journey to Vienna for the purpose meeting Beethoven. He carries some piano sonatas, modeled after those of Beethoven, which he offers to a publisher to earn money to sustain his trip.

33 'Public and Popularity,' chap. 2, in ibid., 6:63.

34 Ibid., 6:65.

35 Ibid, 6:66.

36 Ibid., 6:67. Also, in his article, 'Halévy's "Reine de Chypre",' in Ellis, 7:207, Wagner, in a disguised autobiographical paragraph actually portray's himself as a young man hoping for work writing such popular works.

[The publisher] gave me the advice, however, that if I wanted to some day earn a dollar or so by my compositions, I should begin by making myself a little renommée by gallops and pot-pourris. I shuddered, but my yearning to see Beethoven gained the victory. I composed gallops and pot-pourris, but for the very shame I could never bring myself to cast one glance upon Beethoven in all that time, for fear it should defile him.[37]

In the end, the critical ethical moment for the conductor is which road he takes in a choice which cannot be avoided. In a letter to his patron, Ludwig II of Bavaria in 1865 Wagner explains the choice. 'Music as an art can continue to be merely entertaining and, if so wished, pleasantly gratifying,' or,

> Music as I intend it can and should mean more to this century and to the people of all ages than [a painting by Raphael] could ever mean to that century and to humanity in general.

It is left to him to either 'go completely quiet and disappear completely' or to work in accordance with his beliefs.[38]

So the life of the conductor must often be one of fighting against the tide of mediocrity and the commonplace so comfortable to the general audience. Wagner pictured this as swimming against the stream.

> We might compare it with a river, as to which we must decide whether we will swim against or with its stream. He who swims with it may imagine he belongs to constant progress as it is so easy to be borne along and he never notices that he is being swallowed in the ocean of vulgarity. To swim against the stream must seem ridiculous to those not driven by an irresistible force to the immense exertions that it costs.[39]

Thus it has ever been. The band director today faces the same aesthetic problem faced by his colleagues in the past. On one hand he can welcome the lures of entertainment music, the goal of amusing his public and the instant gratification it brings, although as Wagner warns he will be 'swallowed in the ocean of vulgarity.'

37 'A Pilgrimmage to Beethoven,' in ibid., 7:23.

38 Letter to Ludwig II, Munich, July 5, 1865, in John N. Burk, *Letters of Richard Wagner* (New York: Vienna House, 1972), 648.

39 'The Public in Time and Space,' in Wagner, *Richard Wagner's Prose Works*, 6:94

What then, can the band director learn from this discussion on the ethics of performance? The sad truth is that most university band concert programs which I have heard contain music of little depth. Is there a reason why educational band concerts cannot be aesthetic concerts of art music?

1. Some might say, 'The students are incapable of experiencing profound emotions.' Anyone who believes this has not been paying attention.

2. Some might say, 'The listeners' or 'My listeners are not educated to appreciate art music.' Forty years ago I used to hear high school band directors say, 'My audience won't let me play that kind of music.' Wagner once addressed this topic in a letter to Hans von Bülow,

> I believe an audience should never be criticized; it will always retain the sovereignty of a child. How should it be reproached for its taste? ... We can hope to present ourselves and our higher aims and ... in that way we shall persuade our audiences ... to acquire, without noticing it, a greater refinement of taste.[40]

[40] Letter to Hans von Bülow, Dec. 27, 1868, in Burk, *Letters of Richard Wagner*, 735.

I believe it is delusional to believe an audience who comes to hear an educational performing ensemble, at any level, 'wants' anything in specific before they enter the hall. In past years the very word 'concert' seen on a poster or in some form of advertising carried with it the connotation of aesthetic music and the suggestion that one was not to expect an entertainment event. I must admit that the term 'concert' no longer has any specific meaning and neither does the term 'classical music.' I would recommend as an intellectual beginning point that the conductor must simply be grateful the audience is there. I think he can assume they trust that they have given up an evening for something worthwhile. Beyond that, they leave it to the conductor. The audience should not be assumed to be a barrier.

So what does the conductor do? My first conducting position was at the University of Montana and at that time the population of Montana, which in area is ten per cent larger than Germany, was a little over 600,000 people—half the size of Austin, Texas. Every town in Montana was a small town. When I took the University of Montana Wind Ensemble on concert tours around the state we often played in very small towns and, curiously enough, often had audiences which exceeded the size of the town. So what do you select as repertoire for a small ranching community near the border of Canada, miles from anywhere, a town which rarely experienced live music of any kind? I played Schönberg. And I shall always remember how touched I was when an old rancher, face deeply lined from the exposure to the elements, a man most likely without any university level education, came up after a concert and thanked me for playing Schönberg. He pointed out that it was the first time they had had a chance in this town to hear Schönberg and he clearly took it as a sign of human respect for them on my part. He may have been a rancher far removed from the concert halls of Europe, but he read newspapers all his life and he knew the name. What he really meant was that I brought them something they could not have obtained on their own.

I argue that surely that should be our purpose today. We live in an environment with five hundred channels of TV, radio entertainment, spectator sports of all kinds, cinema which no longer even pretends to be elevated, and so on. Should it be the purpose of the educational institution to provide the public with *more* entertainment? There is no argument whatsoever in support of our doing this. On the contrary, the audience member is prepared genetically to understand music. He is genetically prepared to understand aesthetic music. And like that rancher in Montana, if he isn't provided the opportunity by us, where will he get it?

3. Some say the available repertoire makes it impossible for the educational ensemble, the wind ensemble in particular, to be a valid art medium. Forty years ago, I admit, one had to really dig to find worthy aesthetic music and one often had to resort to chamber music or music from earlier eras in order to fill a year's programs. But today there is literally a world's supply of aesthetic music available. But one still has to spend valuable personal time looking for it. You will not find it walking through the aisles of the publishers at any music education conference. You will not find it in the mails and emails sent you by publishers. What you must do is spend many hours looking at scores where there are pre-selected collections, such as at Shattinger's Music in St. Louis (often represented through the exhibitions by Jim Cochrane) or at a nearby

university band library. There is no short-cut; it is part of the job. But one cannot say there is not enough good aesthetic music available.

4. So, if the problem lies not in the performers, the listeners or in the repertoire, then it is clear the only barrier to the band becoming an art medium must be the band director. The issue could not be more serious for at the individual student level it has to do with character development and taken to its last extremity, nation building. If then the band director chooses to amuse his students and audience instead of moving them, if he chooses to offer them entertainment instead of catharsis, then he must have the honesty to be able to look into a mirror and ask himself, 'What are my ethical and moral responsibilities as a teacher?' 'What have I contributed to the student and to the nation?'

Some may not be pleased with what they see in the mirror. In the 1992 Fall issue of a journal called *Today's Music Educator*, there was published a sad and touching letter to the editor by a man who had been the most famous high school marching band director in Southern California for many years. After retiring from sixty-nine years as a band director he looked back over his own career and came to the conclusion that he had become addicted to applause. He found no one ever questioned his educational values as long as the applause for his marching band continued. But at the end he looked back and found no comfort in what he saw. He asked himself,

> What had I done to prepare my students to become consumers of good music after graduation? When had I given them a preview of the music of the masters? Why had competition become the curriculum of my band?

We shall allow Wagner the final word. First, he warns about the State, or for us the educational systems.

> Why make such a fuss about the falsification of artistic judgment or musical taste? Is it not a mere bagatelle, compared with all the other things we falsify: wares, sciences, victuals, public opinions, State culture awareness, religious dogmas, clover-seed and what not? Are we to grow virtuous all of a sudden in Music? …

The acceptance of the empty for the sound is stunting everything we possess in the way of schools, tuition, academies and so on, by ruining the most natural feelings and misguiding the faculties of the rising generation … But that we should pay for all this and have nothing left when we come to our senses—that, to be frank, is abominable![41]

His judgment on this ethical choice with respect to the individual is even more severe:

The man who strays into the realm of triviality must pay for his transgression at the cost of his own more noble nature. But he who seeks it deliberately, that man is fortunate, for he has *nothing* worth losing.[42]

[41] 'On Poetry and 'Composition,' in Wagner, *Richard Wagner's Prose Works*, 6:146ff.

[42] Letter to Eduard Hanslick, Jan. 1, 1847, in Burk, *Letters of Richard Wagner*, 135.

Wagner on the Art of Conducting

Present-day conductors (many of whom do not even understand the music) the situation at best is as follows: they can identify the key, the theme, the part-writing, the instrumentation, etc., and with that they think they have identified everything that is present in the piece of music.[1]

[1] Letter to Theodor Uhlig, Dresden, Feb. 13, 1852, in John N. Burk, *Letters of Richard Wagner* (New York: Vienna House, 1972), 250.

Wagner's first-hand observation of conductors began in about 1828 when he was fifteen years of age and throughout his life he was very critical of what he heard and saw. A typical example is found in an essay on the German stage. Along with commenting on poor acting and stage business he mentions the problem of finding adequate conductors. He gives an example of a performance he heard in Würzburg of Mozart's *Don Giovanni* which enjoyed surprisingly good singers but had a conductor who seemed intent on showing 'what he could do with even a tempo incorrect throughout.'[2]

[2] This anecdote is found under 'The German Opera-Stage of Today,' in Richard Wagner, *Richard Wagner's Prose Works*, trans. William Ashton Ellis (New York: Broude Brothers, 1966), 5:264.

I learned that the theater management had imported this person from Temesvar, after enticing him from a military band with which he used to arrange very popular garden-concerts.

On the other hand, Wagner notes, it sometimes happens that a theater hires a man with a strong literary background but 'would never be able to learn the beating of time either good or bad.'

Most of his criticism of other conductors, like this example, focus on incorrect tempi but it is easy to see that this is only a metaphor representing his belief that they simply did not understand the score.

On behalf of the men he was so critical of we might remind the reader of what this period represents in the long chronology of conducting. Earlier conductors had been around for a very long time, even with batons. But in nearly every case in earlier centuries they were also the composer and in nearly every case all concerts consisted of brand new music. Our modern concept of a conductor as one who represents the composer was really not possible until the publication of full scores (you really can't study an orchestral work if you don't have a score) and with rehearsal letters (modern rehearsals were not possible until there were rehearsal letters), a time which corresponds with Wagner's early experience in seeing and hearing conductors. So it is perhaps fair to remember that Wagner was criticizing men who were pioneers, the earliest men to find their way toward the role of conducting as we know it.

But there is something even more important. It is easy to imagine that rehearsals in earlier times, when the 'conductor' was the composer and was presiding from his first violin or keyboard desk, that rehearsals consisted of running through the compositions for the purpose of finding mistakes and for the players to find those places where it was expected of them to 'finish' the score. This meant adding more dynamics than were on paper, adding the whole world of expressive playing (none of which is on paper) and the customary improvisation by the individual players. Those court composers who were required to turn out several new major compositions every week depended on this kind of help from the players as a matter of necessity. If there were questions, the composer was there to answer.

The role of the modern conductor is quite different. He understands that his duty is not to reproduce what is on the page, but to study the score until he knows everything which is *not* on the page. First and foremost this means finding the composer's original feeling, none of which can be found on paper as we all are forced to use an ancient notational system in which there is not a single symbol to express emotions. Nothing demonstrates this more clearly than Wagner, during a period of studying the beginning of the *Fifth Symphony* of Beethoven, imagining the great composer's passionate communication with him in regard to a single fermata sign.

> Hold thou my fermata long and terribly! I wrote no fermata for jest or from bepuzzlement, haply to think out my further move; but the same full tone I mean to be squeezed dry in my Adagio [of the 9th Symphony] for utterances of sweltering emotion, I cast among the rushing figures of my passionate Allegro, if need be, a paroxysm of joy or horror. Then shall its life be drained to the last blood drop; then do I part the waters of my ocean, and bare the depths of its abyss; or curb the flocking herd of clouds, dispel the whirling web of mist and open

up a glimpse into the pure blue firmament, the sun's irradiate eye. For this I set fermatas in my Allegros, notes entering of a sudden, and long held out. And mark thou what a definite thematic aim I had with this sustained E-flat, after a storm of three short notes, and what I meant to say by all the like held notes that follow.[3]

3 'On Conducting,' in ibid., 4:312.

That's the kind of communication the modern conductor wants from a score, not the communication with the actual notes on paper, which is precisely why Mahler once famously observed that the important things in music were not found in the notes.

But this is not what Wagner was seeing on the podiums of early nineteenth-century Germany. He was seeing men who seemed more concerned with their image, much like actors, and with being 'in charge.' To symbolize this kind of conductor, Wagner gives us a wonderful and humorous picture of Gaspare Spontini, 1774–1851, who enjoyed far-reaching popularity with his operas while at Berlin, but he left there in 1842, in part, perhaps, due to his egotism, pride and general bad temper.[4] Wagner, however, with his pure artistic perspective admired Spontini as the end of the line of serious opera, *tragédie lyrique*, composers which included Mozart and Gluck. Thereafter, in Wagner's view, all tended toward entertainment.

4 Spontini wrote at least one large scale band work, his *Grosser Sieges- und Festmusik*, ca. 1832, a copy of which can be found with my collection in the Whitwell Archiv, Trossingen, Germany.

When Wagner invited Spontini to Dresden in 1844 the older man was late in life and probably had not expected to be asked to conduct his opera himself. After Wagner invited the guest to take over the rehearsal on the following day Spontini, 'suddenly began to hesitate.'

After a little reflection, he asked me what sort of baton we used for conducting and with my hand I indicated, as near as possible, the length and thickness of a moderate-sized stick of ordinary wood, which the orchestra-attendant served out to us each day wrapped round with fresh white paper.[5] He sighed, and asked me if I thought it feasible to get made for him by the next day a baton of black ebony, of the most portentous length and thickness, which he outlined for me by his arm and hollow hand and bearing at each end a fairly large white knob of ivory. I promised to see to his having at any rate an instrument that should look just like it, for the very next rehearsal, and another made of the precise material he desired, for the performance itself. Surprisingly calmed, he wiped his forehead, gave me permission to announce his acceptance of the direction for the morrow, and departed to his hotel after once more stamping on my memory his requirements in the matter of the baton …

5 This tradition remains in Europe, where the guest conductor will always find a baton lying in wait upon his music stand upon his arrival.

I entered into the minutest details with the stage carpenter about the baton. This turned out so far well, that it had the becoming length and thickness, was black to look on, and bore great knobs of white.[6]

[6] 'Mementoes of Spontini,' Wagner, *Richard Wagner's Prose Works*, 3:129ff.

And at the actual first rehearsal the following day, Wagner recalled,

> In an instant I understood why he had laid so much weight on the baton's form, for he did not take it by one end, like the rest of us conductors, but grasped it fairly in the middle with his whole fist, and manipulated it in a way to show one plainly that he looked on the baton as a marshal's staff and used it, not for beating time with, but commanding.

The reader should be reminded that there was apparently an earlier tradition for holding a baton in this manner, especially among church choir conductors who held a rolled sheet of music, perhaps hastily prepared, to serve as a baton. There are some early engravings which document this, notably one in which J. S. Bach sits at the organ playing with his left hand and wielding a rolled sheet of paper at its mid-point as a baton.

Wagner writes of another demand by Spontini that the oboes be placed directly behind his back. This entire passage will be confusing to the reader unless he recalls that it was a tradition until about 1830 or so for the conductor to face the audience, and not the orchestra. The origin of this custom lay in the days when orchestras were small private ensembles belonging to aristocrats and performing in the large palace rooms. It was thought that if the conductor (and pianists as well in concerti) had their back to the aristocrat it was a sign of lack of respect. It is difficult for us to imagine the loss of eye contact with the orchestra, conducting with the back toward the ensemble, especially in the case of the poor deaf Beethoven.

> I further showed him my devotedness by the zeal with which I carried out an entire re-seating of the orchestra after his own wish. This wish had less to do with system than with habit, and how important it was to him to suffer not the smallest alteration in his habits I clearly saw when he explained to me his method of conducting, for he directed the orchestra—so he said—by a mere glance of his eye,

my left eye is for the first violins, my right for the second violins; wherefore, to work by a glance. One must not wear spectacles as bad conductors do, even if one is short-sighted.

'I,' he admitted confidentially, 'can't see a step before me, and yet I use my eyes in such a way that everything goes as I wish.'

Certain details in the seating to which he had accidentally accustomed himself, in any case were most irrational. Undoubtedly it was from a Paris orchestra of long ago, where some exigency or other had compelled just this arrangement, that the custom dated of placing the two oboe players immediately behind his back. Thus they had to turn the bell of their instruments away from the public's ear, and our excellent oboist was so enraged at this suggestion that it required a particularly jocular treatment of the incident on my part to calm him down for this occasion.[7]

Wagner goes on to explain that the older tradition in Germany was to divide the orchestra on the stage, with all the strings on one side and all the winds on the other, with the conductor standing (facing the audience) in the middle. He suggests that it was during Spontini's visit that they began to spread things around across the stage in the modern fashion. Wagner was delighted with the more blended sound and wanted to maintain this seating plan in Dresden, but it required the king's permission to make such a change. The administration rules!

By the way, in a later account of this period in Dresden, when he conducted the *Ninth Symphony* of Beethoven, he suggests, unfortunately without details, that he had given more thought to the seating of the orchestra.

Moreover I took the precaution of having the platform completely rebuilt, to ensure a good acoustic effect for the orchestra, which I now disposed in an entirely new system.[8]

This may reflect the comments he made in a document relative to the creation of a special orchestra school in 1846. Among his requirements were the principle that 'the width should never be more than twice the depth.'[9]

In his rehearsals Spontini was very demanding in stage business, such as the unison sound of spears dropping on the stage.[10] Of more musical significance was his demand that rhythmic ensemble be achieved through the placement of rhythmic accents. This, in fact, can be a wonderful technique,

[7] 'Mementoes of Spontini, in ibid., 3:134.

[8] 'Choral Symphony at Dresden,' in ibid., 7:245.

[9] Curt von Westernhagen, *Wagner* (London: Cambridge University Press, 1978), 1:90.

[10] 'Mementoes of Spontini,' in Wagner, *Richard Wagner's Prose Works*, 3:131.

and I often asked woodwind players, in passages of fast moving slurred groups to just accent the first note in each group. This invariably immediately eliminates ensemble problems, just as the singer below predicts, 'give due prominence to the first note and the rest would come of itself.' Here is Wagner's discussion of this application by Spontini.

> Characteristic throughout was the energy wherewith he insisted on an often extravagantly acute enunciation of the rhythmic accents. To this end he had accustomed himself, in his rehearsals with the Berlin orchestra, to indicate the to-be-emphasized note by an expression at first incomprehensible to myself, ejaculating '*diese*,' Tichatschek [then a currently famous singer in Germany] a regular genius for the rhythm of song, was particularly delighted by this since he likewise had the habit of spurring the choristers to extra precision, at important entries, by telling them they had only to give due prominence to the first note and the rest would come of itself.[11]

11 Ibid., 135.

There is one more Spontini story which Wagner recalled which I like. I have always encouraged young conductors to use more subjective language to convey the spirit of the music, as opposed to only talking about the left-brain grammar of the notation. Wagner describes such a moment in Spontini's rehearsal of his opera, *Vestale*, although it was an ill-chosen comment as it turned out. A lugubrious aria in Act 2 is accompanied by an eerie figure in the violas. The first stand of violas, in this case two very old gentleman, long past retirement age, looked up in genuine horror at Spontini, believing they had heard an omen, when 'suddenly he turned towards them, and cried with a hollow, graveyard voice, Isn't Death in the violas?'[12]

12 Ibid.

Wagner on the Art of Conducting

Conducting is taught at most universities today as a question of 'How,' but for Wagner everything was centered on the 'What.' It is in Wagner's discussion of this distinction that one finds the quotation quoted at the top of this essay.

> Indeed, the truly absolute musician … could not understand Beethoven any longer, since he was concerned only with the 'How?' and not with the 'What?'; …

For the absolute musician it seemed necessary only to identify the 'How': but it was impossible for him to identify even this correctly, chiefly because he did not understand the 'What' that ought to be expressed by this 'How.' As a result, all contact between conductor and orchestra floundered on a complete lack of understanding between them: the conductor strove to articulate musical phrases which he himself did not understand and which he had made his own rather as one learns melodious verses by heart according to their sound alone when the verses in question are written in a foreign language unknown to the person reciting the poem. In the process, of course, only the most superficial aspects of the work can be taken into account ...

But the conductor who perceives only [the notational aspects of] music in a piece by Beethoven is just like the reciter who sticks only to the language of a poem, or like a person interpreting a painting who sticks only to the colors on the canvas. In the case of present-day conductors (many of whom do not even understand the music) the situation at best is as follows: they can identify the key, the theme, the part-writing, the instrumentation, etc., and with that they think they have identified everything that is present in the piece of music.[13]

[13] Letter to Theodor Uhlig, Dresden, Feb. 13, 1852, in Burk, *Letters of Richard Wagner*, 250.

The *Melos*

The epitome of what Wagner meant in the 'What,' in the above quotation he expressed in a word he coined for this purpose, *melos*, the root of which, of course, was the ancient root for 'melody.' But for Wagner this word also meant everything *expressed* by the melody, the emotional and spiritual communication of the composition.

As mentioned above, Wagner had been suffering for years as a listener hearing performances in which the conductor and orchestra merely played a composition through as it appears on paper. He was particularly struck by the fact that the Paris Conservatoire orchestra, the best then in Europe, studied together the *Ninth Symphony* of Beethoven for three years before playing it in public. The problem was not in the notes, but in finding what Beethoven had in mind. In fact Wagner himself made in his own hand a full score copy as well as a piano transcription fueled by this search. What they were looking for Wagner gave the name 'melos,' leading to the 'true feeling for melodic phrasing.'[14]

[14] In his essay on 'Beethoven's Ninth Symphony,' Wagner gives the flute-oboe passage at bar 407 of the first movement of the *Ninth Symphony* and writes, 'Beyond the nuances already recommended for the *Espressivo*, in every second bar we should have to mark the more strenuous [a hairpin cresc. symbol is given], to do justice to the variation in the *melos*.' To us the implicaton here is merely a stronger drive to the cadence, but this passing *melos* does seem to follow our suggestion that the point is not an analytic perspective of a melody, but how you would sing or make it come alive.

[Habeneck, conductor of the Paris Conservatoire Orchestra] found
the proper tempo, while diligently leading on his orchestra to grasp the sympho-
ny's melos.

The great conductor of the generation after Wagner, Felix
Weingartner (1863–1942), a student of Liszt and later conductor
of the Vienna Philharmonic, made a specific attempt to find
out more about what Wagner meant by *melos* by interviewing musicians who had played under his baton. He arrived at a
definition which is, I think, correct.

> From all we have learned of him as conductor, from himself and from
> others, he obviously aimed in his own performances not only at cor-
> rectness but at bringing out that to which the sounds and notes are only
> the *means*. He sought for the unifying thread, the psychological line, the
> revelation of which suddenly transforms, as if by magic, a more or less
> indefinite sound-picture into a beautifully shaped, heart-moving vision,
> making people ask themselves in astonishment how it is that this work,
> which they had long thought they knew, should have all at once become
> quite another thing, and the unprejudiced mind joyfully confesses, 'Yes,
> thus, *thus*, must it really be.'
>
> Out of the garment of tones there emerges the *spirit of the artwork*; its
> noble countenance, formerly only confusedly visible, is not unveiled,
> and enraptures those who are privileged to behold it. Wagner calls this
> form, this quintessence, this spirit of the artwork its *melos*.[15]

[15] Felix Weingartner, *On Conducting* [1895], trans., Ernest Newman (New York: Kalmus, 1906), 9.

Melody is the vehicle into which all of this is compressed.
Modern clinical research on the brain has made it clear that it
is melody, and not harmony, which carries emotional content.
It is clear from Wagner's comments in his 'Opera and Drama'[16]
that melody itself was his starting point in creating the concept of *melos*.

[16] 'Opera and Drama,' part 1, chap. 7, in Wagner, *Richard Wagner's Prose Works*, 2:103ff.

> We shall quickest reach a lucid survey if we tersely sum up Music's
> nature in the concept of Melody.
>
> …
>
> … so are Harmony and Rhythm indeed the shaping organs, but Melody
> the first real Shape of music.
>
> …
>
> Melody is the most perfect expression of the inner being of Music.
>
> …

With Beethoven we perceive the natural thrust of Life, to free Melody from out music's inner Organism … He sets it before us in all its organic Necessity.

…

True Melody is itself the utterance of an inner organism; to arise organically it must have shaped for itself its very Form and a form entirely adequate to explicitly convey its inner essence.

This kind of language is entirely missing in today's university conducting study, as is discussion of *melos*, and nothing is more rare than a young conductor who even thinks about shaping a melody. As Wagner would have said, we are teaching the 'how' but not the 'what.'

The contemporary teaching of score study is almost entirely objective, consisting of analyzing chords, analyzing forms, etc. This is preferred in the classroom because in a class where each student arrives with a different experiential history the naming of chords, keys and forms are things which all can agree upon. No differing views!

But these things usually emphasized in score study, the analyzing of chords, keys and forms, are really only the grammar of music; Wagner calls them 'lifeless tools.'[17] Their solution will never lead to a satisfactory feeling on the part of the conductor when he asks himself, 'Do I know the score?' Why is this?

Let's think this through. The purpose of music is to communicate emotion.

[1] What could be more obvious than this: the purpose of a performance is to communicate emotion, not to communicate the theory or grammar of music. If the latter were the case we could just hand out copies of the score and dispense with rehearsal and concert.

[2] The challenge to the performer or conductor is to find the *melos*, that universal, experiential, emotional and spiritual message which must be communicated to performers and listeners. It is found in the right hemisphere; theory and grammar are found in the left hemisphere.

[17] 'Zukunftsmusik,' in ibid., 3:296.

So, since we assume the conductor is perfectly capable of understanding the grammar of music, his real challenge is in discovering the experiential and emotional perspective of the composer. If the conductor does not have specific tools to do this, he will sometimes have a block, as described by Wagner,

> But in the Artist, too, the bent to re-present is by its nature thoroughly unconscious, and instinctive. Even where he needs deliberation to shape the picture of his intuition to [a performance] by aid of his own familiar technique, the decisive choice of his expressional means will not be settled by Reflection proper, but rather by an instinctive bent that makes out the very character of his specific gift. The necessity for a lengthy bout of reflection will only come upon him where he stumbles on some great obstacle to the application of the expressional means he needs.[18]

[18] 'Zukunftsmusik,' in ibid., 3:296.

The reason it is so difficult for inexperienced conductors to discover the important truths in a score is due to a little gift to us from the medieval Roman Church. They gave us (intentionally) a notational system in which there is not a single symbol of any kind having to do with feeling. The Church taught music as a branch of arithmetic and they gave us an arithmetic notational system. The church was trying to eliminate emotions from the lives of the early Christians and so in school they taught only the arithmetic of music and left everything else to the musicians on the street to take care of. Performance practice itself changed this concept of music but the educational world has always been far behind.

Ironically, it is the public 'who knows nothing' who understands the true meaning of music. Uninfluenced by the educational world's emphasis on the grammar of music, the public always understands the true language of music, the communication of emotions, because they come prepared from birth to do exactly that by virtue of genetic knowledge. And this is exactly why Wagner once observed,

> It is the non-musician who has led the way to a true understanding of Beethoven's work.'[19]

[19] Letter to Theodor Uhlig, Dresden, Feb. 13, 1852, in Burk, *Letters of Richard Wagner*, 250.

Although Wagner did not have access to the findings of modern clinical research regarding the genetic understanding of music, in particular of melody, he was aware that man has both the ability to communicate to others and to understand communication from others.

> Man is in a two-fold way a poet: in his *beholding* and in his *imparting*. His natural poetic-gift is the faculty of condensing into an inner image the phenomena presented to his senses from outside. His *artistic*, that of projecting this image outwards.[20]

[20] 'The Play and Dramatic Poetry,' part 2, in Wagner, *Richard Wagner's Prose Works*, 2:152.

It is this which makes possible the most significant aspect of performance. The orchestra or band discovers and projects outward the epitome, or what Schopenhauer called the quintessence, of an emotion. This is what reaches the ear of the listener, but then this form of the emotion is automatically processed by the listener's own 'experience base' which sifts that emotion until it achieves a correspondence with the listeners own personal experience with that emotion. Hence music communicates on both a general and an individual level at all times. This is what Wagner was thinking when he wrote,

> What Music expresses is eternal, infinite and ideal. She expresses not the passion, love or desire of this or that individual in this or that condition, but Passion, Love and Desire itself, and in such infinitely varied phases as lie in her unique possession and are foreign and unknown to any other tongue. Of her let each man taste according to his strength, his faculty and mood, what taste and feeling he can.[21]

[21] 'A Happy Ending,' in ibid., 7:81.

For Wagner the concept of *melos* was inseparable from tempo. But look how he thinks of tempo: 'the *right tempo* had to be found for its *every beat*.' This statement, and the following, reveal the primary distinction between the concept of tempo by great artists and that taught by schools. I would put it this way: Tempo is not found in the score; it is found in the music. Wagner, continued as follows:

> [Habeneck, conductor of the Paris Conservatoire Orchestra] *found the proper tempo, while diligently leading on his orchestra to grasp the symphony's melos.*
>
> *But a correct conception of the melos alone can give the proper tempo: the two are indivisible; one conditions the other.*

It is on this point that Wagner is most critical of the common professional conductors he had heard in Germany.

> I do not scruple to declare that by far the most performances of our classic instrumental works are seriously inadequate. I propose to substantiate my verdict by pointing out that *our conductors know nothing of proper Tempo, because of their understanding nothing about Song*. I have never met a single German Kapellmeister or musical conductor who could really *sing* a melody (let his voice be good or bad). No, Music to them is an abstraction, a cross between syntax, arithmetic and gymnastics; so that one may well conceive its votaries making capital teachers at a conservatoire or musical high school, but never imagine them breathing life and soul into a musical performance.

In continuing his remarks on tempi, Wagner stresses that only study will reveal tempo and if this fails to 'divine the music's character and expression, what will it profit the conductor to be given an Italian sign of tempo?' I might point out that Leopold Mozart wrote in 1756 that the meaning of these familiar Italian words at the beginning of the score had by that date already been lost. Wagner also points to the futility of the metronome.

> To speak from my very own experience, I may state that I furnished my earlier operas ... with downright eloquent directions for tempo and fixed them past mistaking (as I thought) by metronomic numbers. But whenever I heard a foolish tempo in a performance of my *Tannhäuser*, for instance, my recriminations were always parried by the plea that my metronomic marks had been followed most scrupulously.
>
> So I saw how uncertain must be the value of mathematics in music, and thenceforth dispensed with the metronome; contenting myself with quite general indications for even the first measure, and devoting all my forethought to its *modifications*, since our conductors know as good as nothing of the latter.

His final sentence here is very near to a note Beethoven wrote on one of his autograph scores,

> 100 according to Maelzel; but this must be held applicable to only the first measures, for feeling also has its tempo and this cannot entirely be expressed in this figure.[22]

[22] Quoted in Erich Leinsdorf, *The Composer's Advocate* (New Haven: Yale University Press, 1981), 165.

And again,

> As to the tempi … I here can only say that if conductor and singers are to depend for their time-measure on the metronomical marks alone, the spirit of their work must stand indeed in sorry case.[23]

[23] 'The Performing of Tannhäuser,' in Wagner, *Richard Wagner's Prose Works*, 3:190.

Another criticism which Wagner finds in most of the conductors he knew was their failure to understand, through the nature of the music itself, those places where one should, in order to clarify melodic shaping, conduct not the quarter-notes which appear on paper, but half-notes. Very much of the music from Mozart through Gounod have this characteristic, that they are often conducted in a different meter than they were written for ease in reading the notation. Wagner addresses this problem as follows:

> To be sure, I now am speaking of the thorough bunglers, people who have an uncommon dread of the *alla breve* beat and always abide by four strictly measured quarter-note strokes per bar, apparently to keep awake their consciousness that they're conducting to some purpose. How these four-footed creatures ever jumped from their village churches to our opera houses, God only knows.

Wagner continues his discussion of tempo with charming examples of occasions where the music was performed too fast or too slow. Always, however, he comes back to studying the score to find the emotions which determine the correct, natural and universal-feeling of tempo. In two sentences, for example, he uses the words 'horror,' 'despair,' 'dignity,' 'mystery of awe' and 'passion.'[24] These kinds of words are in harmony with Wagner's concept as an expression of the *melos*. The academic world stands in virtual horror at the thought of teaching tempo in this fashion, even though every singer in the world does exactly this.

[24] 'About Conducting,' in ibid., 4:327.

On Conducting Gestures

It is clear that Wagner's concept of conducting gestures follows his basic themes. First, he says, the gestures follow what he called 'Nature's Necessity.' By this he meant that the gestures must represent the internal understanding of the emotions in the music and not the outer symbols, the notation.

> Man will never be that which he can and should be, until his Life is a true mirror of Nature, a conscious following of the only real Necessity, *the inner natural necessity*, and is no longer held in subjugation to an *outer* artificial counterfeit,—which is thus no necessary, but an arbitrary power.[25]

[25] 'The Art-Work of the Future,' in ibid., 1:71

He mentions this again in the same essay, now sounding very much as if he were addressing the graduate conducting class!

> Man's nature is twofold, an *outer* and an *inner*. The senses by which he offers himself to the observer as a subject for Art, are those of *Vision* and of *Hearing*: to the eye appeals the outer man, the inner to the ear …
>   The corporeal man and the spontaneous expression of his sensations of physical anguish or well-being [happiness], called up by outward contact, appeal directly to the eye, while indirectly he imparts to it, by means of facial play and gesture, those emotions of the inner man which are not directly understood by the (observer's) eye … The more distinctly can the outer man express the inner, the higher does he show his rank as an artistic being.
>   But the inner man can only find *direct* communication through the ear, and that by means of *his voice's music*. Music is the immediate utterance of feeling … Through the sense of hearing, music urges forth from the feeling of one heart to the feeling of [another].[26]

[26] 'The Art-Work of the Future,' in ibid., 1:91

Since the concepts of movement and music have been so closely related ever since the time of ancient man, it is no surprise that Wagner brings dance into the discussion. His discussion of dance, in his 'Art-Work of the Future,' is of a more primitive sense better expressed by 'movement,'[27] and some of his discussion pertains directly with the conductor's movements. He considers movement, music and poetry as fundamentally characteristic of ancient man. Poetry only here because he fancied himself a poet; certainly speech had no role in early man, but comes much later. It is interesting that Wagner associates singing with movement, no doubt because

[27] This discussion begins in ibid., 'The Art-Work of the Future,' 1:100.

singing always is a faithful voice of the experiential side of our selves. The description is still very close to a description of a good conductor's gestures.

> The singing man ... must necessarily be a bodily man; through his outer form, through the posture of his limbs, the inner, singing ... man comes forth to view.

In his discussion of dance, Wagner makes a parenthetical comment that at the service of entertainment dance has degenerated from being a reflection of the entire person to just becoming a function of the feet. Today, he says, 'head, neck, trunk and thighs are only present as unbidden guests.' This, he says, explains the 'woodenness of civilized vapidity' found in social dancing, such as in Balls. Now it is only the ballerina that we permit to express the 'frankest candor' in her gestures as she 'stands above the law.' We allow ourselves to be incited by her, without any intention of following her in our moral life. Just, he adds, as while Religion offers us invitations to goodness and to virtue, 'yet we are not in the smallest [degree] bound to yield to them in everyday existence.'[28]

Returning to his topic of movement, Wagner says that rhythm is the repetition of these movements expressing the inner man (feeling). What he next writes is the most fundamental reason why time is found in the music (within) and not on the page (in the score) and at the same time should be the goal of every conductor.

> It is the conscious soul of those necessitated movements by which he strives instinctively to impart to others his own emotions.[29]

In the following the subject was the Drama, but if you substitute the word Conductor for Drama he makes the same point,

> In Drama, therefore, an action can only be explained when it is completely vindicated by the Feeling; and it thus is the dramatic poet's task, not to invent actions, but to make an action so intelligible through its emotional Necessity, that we may altogether dispense with the intellect's assistance in its vindication.[30]

[28] 'The Art-Work of the Future,' in ibid., 1:106ff.

[29] 'The Art-Work of the Future,' in ibid., 101

[30] 'Opera and Drama,' part 2, chap. 4, in ibid., 2:209.

On the Rehearsal

It is a truth forever, that
where the speech of man stops short,
there Music's reign begins.[31]

31 'A Happy Evening,' in ibid., 7:73.

In that statement we have not only the physical truth of the
bicameral mind, but the essential dilemma of the rehearsal
environment. Language is just as inadequate in discussing
music as it is in discussing love, or any other quality associated
with the right hemisphere of the brain. We know better and
yet we talk.

Wagner knew better and yet his need to describe the *melos*
was so urgent that it was in the form of an apology that he
confessed, 'I must add that my principal remarks were made by
word of mouth at the rehearsals.'

He was particularly concerned in the example of singers,
the only musicians who use words in performance. There we
have a real struggle between language and music, between the
left and right hemispheres of the brain. It was Wagner's habit,
therefore, to have reading rehearsals before the regular rehearsals with the orchestra. In 1852 in an essay, 'On the Performing
of *Tannhäuser*,' Wagner explains that after the score has been
mailed to the singers in advance, that he would next have a
'vocal rehearsal.' What he meant by this was having the singers gather together to *read*, not sing, their parts, with Wagner
demanding the proper emotional expression in their reading. Without this, it was his experience that the singers would
only be concerned with their own private vocal technique
and would never achieve the personification of the charac-
ters which make an opera come to life as a living drama. He
did the same thing with the chorus, a rehearsal to read with
the expression of professional actors before the first singing
rehearsal. If the directors are not willing to do this, Wagner recommends, then put the score on the shelf and forget
the production.[32]

32 'The Performing of Tannhäuser,' in ibid., 3:172ff.

The reason Wagner found this so effective we understand
today following decades of clinical research in brain function. We understand today that language is in the left hemisphere of the brain, but exists there like a dictionary—with no

expression whatsoever. It is the right-hemisphere which adds emotional emphasis to the spoken language and it is *only* this emotional emphasis which creates *meaning*. It works like this:

'I ate a hotdog.'
'*I* ate a hotdog' [as opposed to someone else ate it]
'I *ate* a hotdog.' [as opposed to throwing it at someone]
'I ate *a* hotdog.' [as opposed to eating two]
'I ate a *hotdog*.' [as opposed to eating a hamburger]

One can also create variations of this in instrumental rehearsals, by having a section playing a unison melody, for example, emphasize different melodic notes. The results will be immediately apparent to the students and due to the genetic qualities of the emotions the students will always prefer the same version you do. Doing this through language ('the fourth note should be 15% louder than …') takes much more time and almost never works because players in rehearsal tend to ignore spoken remarks. The student players are in a right-hemisphere experiential mode and the spoken instructions by the conductor come from his left-hemisphere. He might as well address them in Russian. It is for this reason that most conductors quickly learn to sing their instructions whenever possible.[33] Wagner makes the same point in another place.

> Even today, albeit we have accustomed ourselves to a most minute notation of the nuances of phrasing, the more talented conductor often finds himself obliged to teach his ensemble members very weighty, but delicate shadings of expression by *vivâ voce* explanation; and these communications, as a rule, are better understood and heeded, than the written signs.[34]

We have two anecdotes regarding Wagner's comments to the orchestra in rehearsal which were recalled regarding the rehearsal of Beethoven's *Ninth Symphony* before its performance on the day of the laying of the corner stone for the new theater in Bayreuth. In both examples he was focused on the character of the passage being rehearsed. First, when the singer stood to sing the famous phrase, '*O friends, not these tones,*' Wagner cried, 'with more spirit, as if you meant to say, 'What awful rubbish you fellows are playing!'

33 As a conducting student at the University of Michigan I was told never to sing in rehearsal. Their argument was that if you had to sing it meant you did not really understand what you wanted, for if you really knew what you wanted you could explain it in words. Ignorance is also found in high places.

34 'A Music School for Munich,' in Wagner, *Richard Wagner's Prose Works*, 4:192.

On this occasion the players, all chosen by Wagner, came from orchestras throughout Germany. The timpanist, Henschel, was a well-known member of the Berlin Royal Orchestra. In the *fortissimo* passage just before the choral Finale, Wagner called to him excitedly, 'My dear Henschel! Imagine that the combined timpani of the whole world are to be heard in this passage. Play way as if the devil were after you!'[35]

This was a private performance so to the musicians Wagner explained,

> There will be no program, no announcements to be read on the street corners; we are giving no concert, only making music for our own enjoyment and to show the world how Beethoven should be played, and may the devil take anyone who criticizes us!

Perhaps it was problems with the English language which caused him some particular disappointment in communicating with an orchestra in London in 1855. He writes to Liszt,

> I have stepped right into a morass of etiquette and custom and am in it up to my ears, unable to channel even a drop of fresh water in my direction in order to revive myself. 'Sir, we are not used to that sort of thing here.' – that is all I ever hear, perpetually echoed back at me! Not even the orchestra can offer me any compensation: it consists almost entirely of Englishmen, et., skilled machines whom I can never really get going: trade and business stifle every other emotion. Added to this is a public which – I am generally assured – is very well-disposed towards me but which can never be drawn out of itself: it sits through the most moving music as it does through the most boring, without ever betraying the fact that it has received any real impression. And then there is this ridiculous Mendelssohn-cult, the whole brazen hypocrisy of this absurd nation.[36]

'Music is the speech of Passion,'[37] and he found none in London. And it was this frustration which caused him to reject an invitation which came at this very time to travel to America.

35 Caroline V. Kerr, *The Bayreuth Letters of Richard Wagner* (New York: Vienna House, 1972), 94.

36 Letter to Liszt from London, May 16, 1855, in Burk, *Letters of Richard Wagner*, 341.

37 'Judaism in Music,' in Wagner, *Richard Wagner's Prose Works*, 3:86.

Part 2
On the Woodwind Instruments

On The Woodwind Instruments

BECAUSE WAGNER'S EARLIEST INTRODUCTION to wind instruments came from hearing military bands on the street, there runs through his writings a certain hesitation about them, as represented by his observation,

> We have agreed that nothing is more prosaic and upsetting, than the hideous aspect of the swollen cheeks and puckered features of the wind players…[1]

Even when listening indoors he seems to expect a certain lack of control.

> In such moods my otherwise scrupulous musical ear is complaisant enough to allow even the quack of an oboe to cause me but a momentary twinge; with an indulgent smile I let the false note of a trumpet graze my ear, without being torn from the blessed feeling that cheats me into the belief that I am hearing the most consummate execution of my favorite work.[2]

The period of Wagner's youth and early music education corresponded with a period in the history of the orchestra when there were dramatic changes in the manufacture of wind instruments and as well a period of ever increasing string sections. As might be expected, Wagner, as a listener, was frequently aware of balance problems. An example is the sudden change in the developments in the horn, as it moved from its eighteenth century natural horn history to the modern design with valves. He mentions this as a matter of caution in his essay on conducting, after hearing a performance of the overture to Spohr's *Jessonda*.

> Not that everything here was as it should be: the passages for the woodwinds were taken a shade too tamely; on the other hand the horn's first solo was blown too loud, and with a perceptible taint of affectation—in which I recognized the failing common to all our hornists since the invention of the ventil-horn.[3]

[1] 'A Happy Evening,' in Richard Wagner, *Richard Wagner's Prose Works*, trans. William Ashton Ellis (New York: Broude Brothers, 1966), 7:70.

[2] 'A Happy Evening,' in ibid., 7:71.

[3] 'About Conducting,' in ibid., 6:6.

Wagner was particularly sensitive to the balance of winds and strings in the music of Beethoven, where the fewer number of woodwinds were not under-weighted in orchestras with larger string sections.

> As an instance of my pains to secure distinctness I may cite a passage of the second movement, at first in C, where the whole of the strings maintain the principal rhythmic figure, in a unison of three octaves, against the second theme allotted to the weak woodwinds. *Fortissimo* is prescribed for the whole orchestra, carry it out as you will, the melody of the woodwinds is completely lost in what really is nothing but a string accompaniment, and as good as never heard at all.[4]

His practical solution was to begin to double the wind parts and request of the strings 'a mere suggestion of strength.' His concern led to an essay on such changes in the winds of the *Ninth Symphony* of Beethoven, which brought him immediate hostile criticism.

Even within the wind choir he was bothered by the imbalance between woodwinds and the brass, reminding his readers that Beethoven was forced to use natural trumpets and horns which simply did not have all necessary melodic tones available.

> True, that Beethoven succeeds at times in giving the woodwinds the necessary incisiveness, through allying them with the brass. But he was so lamentably hampered by the structure of the 'natural' horns and trumpets, the only ones then known, that their employment to reinforce the woodwinds has been the very cause of those perplexities which we feel as irremovable obstacles to the plan emergence of the melody.[5]

His solution, now that he had brass instruments which could play 'all' the notes, was to rewrite the old parts and add the notes which Beethoven was forced to leave out. In discussing the ethics involved in making such changes in the score, Wagner gives us a wonderful phrase to refer to those notes the brass could not play and which the audience never heard.

> The question is whether one prefers to go for some time without hearing anything of the composer's intentions distinctly, or to adopt the best expedient for doing justice to them. In this respect the audience of our concert halls and opera houses is certainly accustomed to quite unconscious act of self-denial.[6]

[4] 'Choral Symphony at Dresden,' in ibid., 7:244. Traditional books on the history of the orchestra sometimes suggest that it was the increased interest in wind manufacture which forced the string sections to become larger in order to compete. This quotation by Beethoven suggests it may have been the other way around.

[5] 'Beethoven's Ninth Symphony,' in ibid., 5:234.

[6] Ibid., 5:239.

In his various prose writings, Wagner rarely discusses individual wind instruments in great detail. However, in several more general discussions of the winds of the orchestra, one can see glimpses of that thorough knowledge of all the winds which is so clearly demonstrated in his music. For example, in his essay on conducting, Wagner addresses the question of balance, and in particular the importance of the fully sustained tone as the basis for tonal power.

> But, since our modern conductors know almost nothing of this, they plume themselves instead on an *over-hushed piano*. Now, this is attainable by the strings without much effort, but it costs a great deal to the winds, especially the woodwinds. From the latter, and above all the flautists, who have turned their once so gentle instruments into veritable tubes of violence, a delicately sustained piano is hardly to be obtained any more—save perhaps from French oboists, as they never transgress the pastoral character of their instrument, or from clarinetists when one asks them for the echo effect. This evil, to be encountered in our very best orchestras, suggests the question: If the wind players are really incapable of a smooth piano, why doesn't one try at least to maintain a balance, and make the strings replace their often positively laughable contrast by a somewhat fuller body of tone?[7]

7 'About Conducting,' in ibid., 4:313.

In 1840 Wagner published a review of a *Stabat Mater* of Pergolesi, which had been rescored for a larger, modern orchestra by the Russian composer, Alexis Lvoff. Wagner felt Lvoff made his arrangement generally with 'discretion beyond all praise,' except for a few passages, such as one in which, 'it was wrong, perhaps, to transfer the part of the violins to the bassoons and clarinets.'[8]

8 'Perolesi's Stabat Mater,' in ibid., 7:104ff.

In another place, Wagner criticizes the French composer, Halévy, for his use of woodwinds in his *Reine de Chypre*. The criticism itself reflects as well the problem of the rapidly increasing size of the nineteenth-century orchestra. Halévy, Wagner says,

> has fallen into the fault of asking from clarinets and oboes an effect to be expected of nothing but horns and ventil-trumpets; and thus it comes, that these passages give one the impression of a thorough schoolboy's instrumentation.[9]

9 'Halévys Reine de Chypre,' in ibid., 7:221.

Wagner held out the model of Mozart as an instance where a composer changed the instrumentation of an earlier master-piece, in this case the Handel *Messiah*.

> Is it not permissible to assume that the composer, unacquainted with the more perfect modern use of the winds employed the organ to produce the same effects that Mozart entrusted later to the improved wind instruments of his day?
>
> ...
>
> [On Mozart's additions] Three trombones, two trumpets, the drums, two clarinets and two bassoons—such are the elements added to the original orchestra. And most frequently it is only the clarinets and bassoons that take an active part in the accompaniment, following the precedent of the bassoons and basset horns in his *Requiem*.[10]

The Flute

In a very early letter (15 June 1832) to the music publisher, Schott, we find the curious request for a score of Johann Hummel's arrangement of the first seven Beethoven symphonies for flute, violin, cello, and piano. Undoubtedly Wagner was interested in seeing these as a model for some similar notion to raise money (in the same letter he sent this publisher his own piano arrangement of the *Ninth Symphony*, requesting that it be considered for publication). Indeed, we know that by 1841, when he was living in Paris, he had arranged the music of the overture to *La Favorita* for violin or flute with piano. This comes to our attention in an anecdote Wagner gives in his autobiography. In an apartment next to his lived a pianist who practiced all day long Liszt's piano fantasie on *Lucia di Lammermoor*. One day, to teach the neighbor a lesson, Wagner had a flutist friend, named Brix, bring his piccolo and the two of them played this *La Favorita* arrangement with the piano against the wall. The neighbor moved out the next day.[11]

Another specific reference in which Wagner singles out the flute family in his prose literature is a passage in which he expressed disdain, as he often did, for the popular music he heard in Paris.

[10] 'Pergolesi's Stabat Mater,' in ibid., 7:104.

[11] Richard Wagner, *My Life* (New York: Tudor, 1911), 237.

So, once more, praise be to music, and also to the happy fact that the Parisians have unanimously decided to adopt music as one of their amusements! Music is the means by which we Germans can come to understand Paris fully, and with its help we can count on grasping its secrets, from the flageolet tones of the singer Duprez down to the genuine flageolets of the balls in the Rue St Honore.[12]

The Oboe

When Wagner was living in Paris in 1840, his financial situation forced him, among other things, to write articles and reviews for newspapers. Among these efforts was a charming fictional account of a German composer, identified only as 'R,' and his pilgrimage to visit Beethoven. A sequel, written in 1841, describes an outdoor evening concert which left our composer in such a pleasant mood that even his otherwise, 'scrupulous musical ear is complaisant enough to allow even the quack of an oboe to cause me but a momentary twinge.'[13] Another installment tells of the death of this composer in Paris. As he lies dying, he speaks of the kinds of bureaucratic humiliations which Wagner had experienced in what the composer calls 'the Ante-chambers of Hunger,' in attempting to arrange performances. In his dying account, the fictional composer recalls a 'ghost-like' oboe tone. It vividly reminds one of the long oboe note which begins the Adagio of the *Gran Partita*, K. 361, of Mozart.

> In those Ante-chambers I dreamed away a fair year of my life. I dreamt of many wondrous mad and fabled stories from the 'Thousand-and-one Nights,' of men and beasts, of gold and offal. My dreams were of gods and contrabassists, of jeweled snuffboxes and prima-donnas, of satin gowns and lovesick lords, of chorus-girls and five-franc pieces. Between I sometimes seemed to hear the wailing, ghost-like note of an oboe; that note thrilled through my every nerve, and cut my heart. One day when I had dreamed my maddest, and that oboe note was tingling through me at its sharpest, I suddenly awoke and found I had become a madman. At least I recollect, that I had forgotten to make my usual obeisance to the theatre-lacky as I left the anteroom,—the reason, I may add, of my never daring to return to it; for *how* would the man have received me?[14]

[12] 'The Opera Lies Dying,' written February 23, 1841, for the *Dresden Abendzeitung*.

[13] 'A Happy Evening,' in Wagner, *Richard Wagner's Prose Works*, 7:71.

[14] 'An End in Paris,' in ibid., 7:61.

During the Fall of 1844, Wagner invited Spontini to Dresden to participate in the production of the latter's *Vestale*. Spontini was by this time an older man and exhibited many eccentric characteristics, which Wagner says, 'stamped themselves so sharply in my memory.' Wagner wrote an account of this visit for publication in his complete prose works in 1851, which included a description of Spontini's change of the orchestra's seating plan. One can only assume from this account that Spontini was still conducting facing the audience, a tradition based on an older social custom under which one did not turn one's back on the aristocracy.

> Spontini showed obvious discontent with his position relative to the orchestra, and before all things wished the oboes placed behind his back. Since this single change would momentarily have called up great confusion in the seating of the orchestra, I promised to arrange it for him after the rehearsal …
>
> Certain details in the seating to which he had accidentally accustomed himself, in any case were most irrational; undoubtedly it was from a Paris orchestra of long ago, where some exigency or other had compelled just this arrangement, that the custom dated of placing the two oboe players immediately behind his back. Therefore they had to turn the bell of their instruments away from the public's ear, and our excellent oboist was so enraged at this suggestion that it required a particularly jocular treatment of this incident, on my part, to calm him down for this occasion.[15]

[15] 'Mementoes of Spontini,' in ibid., 3:131ff.

The only oboist Wagner mentions by name is a man named, Fries, who was the principal oboist of the Zurich orchestra.

> He had to practice with me, just as a singer would do, the more important parts allotted to his instrument in Beethoven's symphonies. When we first produced the Symphony in C minor, this extraordinary man played the small passage marked adagio at the fermata of the first movement in a manner I have never heard equaled. After my retirement from the directorship of these concerts, he left the orchestra and went into business selling music.[16]

[16] Wagner, *My Life*, 553.

Wagner mentions this same passage, the famous oboe *eingang* in the recapitulation of the first movement of the *Fifth Symphony*, in his essay on conducting. Here he gives us a somewhat enigmatic commentary on the interpretation of this passage.

> The best hints I ever had for the tempo and phrasing of Beethoven's music were those I once derived from the soulful, sure-accented singing of the great Schroder-Devrient; it has since been impossible for me to

allow the affecting cadenza [sic] for the oboe in the first movement of the C minor Symphony to be dragged in the way I have always heard elsewhere. No, harking back from this cadenza itself, I also found the meaning and expression for that prolonged fermata of the first violins in the same passage and the stirring impression I gained from this pair of insignificant looking points gave me a new insight into the life of the whole movement.[17]

[17] 'About Conducting,' in Wagner, *Richard Wagner's Prose Works*, 4:298.

The Clarinet

The one clarinet player who Wagner discusses in his prose literature, was one Mr. Ott-Imhoff, a member of the Zurich orchestra. He was, writes Wagner,

> a highly cultured and well to do man who belonged to a noble family and had joined the orchestra as a patron and as an amateur musician. He played the clarinet with a soft and charming tone which was somewhat lacking in spirit.[18]

[18] Wagner, *My Life*, 554.

The Bassoon

In a letter of 1848 to the music director at Riga, Wagner mentions a bassoonist, unfortunately not by name, who left for greater opportunities in America.

> I, for my part, tell you frankly that if I were a poor performing musician I would not go to America now, for the simple reason that I should have been there long ago. What slavery is the lot of us poor musicians over here! I can see no grounds for dissuading any one from seeking his fortune there, where he is more likely to find it under any circumstances than here. If I cared to give instances, I could mention a case that lately became known here of a bassoonist who went to America as a poor man, and in a very short time sent for his wife and children, as he had received a $1500 situation.

During his conducting engagement in London in 1855, Wagner mentions his high regard for the wind players there, and especially the bassoons.

> These musicians have the *ability* to do anything: the wind section in particular, is very good, and there is of course no question of my suffering the sort of torment I had to put up with in Zurich, since the *bassoons*, too, are excellent.[19]

[19] Letter to Minna Wagner, March 13, 1855.

Part 3

On the Brass and Percussion Instruments

On the Brass and Percussion Instruments

IN ADDITION TO THE COMMENTS on various members of the brass family, there is an interesting discussion by Wagner on the use of horns and trumpets in the Beethoven symphonies. First, because Beethoven was so 'lamentably hampered by the structure of the "natural" horns and trumpets,' Wagner believed in certain patterns of rewriting these parts for use by modern instruments for the purpose of more logical balance and support. He even allowed the addition of trumpets where not written by Beethoven, if the need were to strengthen a wind line and if the only alternative were to force the rest of the orchestra to play softer.[1]

In a different discussion of the nature of the opera overture, Wagner speaks of the importance of the instrumentation reflecting what the listener would associate with real life. He gives, as excellent examples, 'the use of the trombones of the Priests in the *Magic Flute*, the trumpet signal in *Leonora*, and the call of the magic horn in *Oberon*.'[2]

Wagner never hesitated to insult his friends and so one is not surprised to find his criticism of the use of brass in a work sent to him by Hans von Bülow in 1854. In this case, which is valuable for its insight on how he heard the treatment of brass in general at this time, Wagner found the music,

> does not strike me as being in any way remarkable, but seems rather bombastic, after the fashion in which composers regularly write when they are not really sure what to make of a given poetic motif.[3]

Wagner was also observant of the reaction by the audience to various instruments, as this eternal comment reveals:

> I remember noticing people who never stirred a muscle when a brass instrument really went wrong, but stopped their ears the instant they saw the wretched player shake his head in shame and confusion.[4]

[1] 'Beethoven's Ninth Symphony,' in Richard Wagner, *Richard Wagner's Prose Works*, trans., William Ashton Ellis, (New York: Broude Brothers, 1966), 5:234ff.

[2] 'On the Overture,' in ibid., 7:163.

[3] Letter to Hans von Bülow, October 26, 1854.

[4] 'A Happy Evening,' in Wagner, *Richard Wagner's Prose Works*, 7:72.

The Trumpet

There is one early reference to the trumpet which is quite interesting. As a young conductor in 1833, Wagner was learning new works for his opera repertoire. Two of these he mentions were the *Vampir* by Marschner and the very popular *Robert the Devil*, by Meyerbeer. Of the Meyerbeer, Wagner writes,

> The score of *Robert* was a great disappointment to me: from the newspapers I had expected plenty of originality and novelty; I could find no trace of either in this transparent work ... The only thing that impressed me was the unearthly keyed trumpet which, in the last act, represented the voice of the mother's ghost.[5]

[5] Richard Wagner, *My Life* (New York: Tudor, 1911), 89.

Two years later, in 1835, Wagner composed his *Columbus Overture* and as he recalls this in his autobiography he seems almost excited about his use of trumpets.

> When the whole had been repeated, there was a sudden jump to a different theme in extreme pianissimo, accompanied by the swelling vibrations of the first violins, which was intended to represent a *Fata Morgana*. I had secured three pairs of trumpets in different keys, in order to produce this exquisite, gradually dawning and seductive theme with the utmost niceties of shade and variety of modulation. This was intended to represent the land of desire towards which the hero's eyes are turned ... My six trumpets were now to combine in one key, in order that the theme assigned to them might re-echo in glorious jubilation. Familiar as I was with the excellence of the Prussian regimental trumpeters, I could rely upon a startling effect, especially in this concluding passage.[6]

[6] Ibid., 119.

Shortly after this performance, Wagner scheduled another on a program that also included a performance of Beethoven's *Wellington's Victory*. The victory, Wagner writes, was one of the orchestra over the audience!

> But, alas! another and more unexpected mishap befell my concert, through the unfortunate selection of music ... My *Columbus Overture*, with its six trumpets, had early in the evening filled the audience with terror; and now, at the end, came Beethoven's *Schlacht bei Vittoria*, for which, in enthusiastic expectation of limitless receipts, I had provided every imaginable orchestral luxury. The firing of cannon and musketry was organized with the utmost elaboration ... while the trumpets and bugles had been doubled and trebled. Then began a battle, such as has seldom been more cruelly fought in a concert hall. The orchestra flung

itself, so to speak, upon the scanty audience with such an overwhelming superiority of numbers that the latter speedily gave up all thought of resistance and literally took to flight.[7]

In 1838, after Wagner had moved to Riga, he programmed the *Columbus Overture* again together with a new work, the *Rule Britannia Overture*. This time, however, he was disappointed.

I myself had not taken any pleasure in the performance of either of these overtures, as my predilection for cornets, strongly marked in both these overtures, again played me a sorry trick, as I had evidently expected too much of our Riga musicians, and had to endure all kinds of disappointment on the occasion of the performance.[8]

But, a much greater disappointed awaited Wagner in Paris during the Winter of 1839–1840.

When I went to fetch the score of [the *Columbus Overture*] from Habeneck, who had it stored among the archives of the Conservatoire, he warned me somewhat dryly, though not without kindness, of the danger of presenting this work to the Parisian public, as, to use his own words, it was too 'vague.' One great objection was the difficulty of finding capable musicians for the six cornets required, as the music for this instrument, so skillfully played in Germany, could hardly, if ever, be satisfactorily executed in Paris. Herr Schlitz, the corrector of my 'Suites' for Cornet a piston, offered his assistance. I was compelled to reduce my six cornets to four, and he told me that only two of these could be relied on.

As a matter of fact, the attempts made at the rehearsal to produce those very passages on which the effect of my work chiefly depended were very discouraging. Not once were the soft high notes played but they were flat or altogether wrong …

I was told later that my overture, however wearisome it had been, would certainly have been applauded if those unfortunate cornet players, by continually failing to produce the effective passages, had not excited the public to almost the point of hostility; for Parisians, for the most part, care only for the skillful parts of performances, as, for instance, for the faultless production of difficult tones. I was clearly conscious of my complete failure.[9]

During 1840–1841, while living in Paris, Wagner was forced to turn to writing newspaper articles and arranging music for local publishers in order to generate income. One of the projects he accepted, and always looked back on with some discomfort, was arranging opera arias for the cornet, then an instrument of great popularity in Paris. He gives a detailed account of this work in his autobiography.

> I now began to work diligently on the composition of *Rienzi*, although, to my great distress, I had often to interrupt this work in order to undertake certain pot-boiling hack-work for Schlesinger.
>
> As my contributions to the *Gazette Musicale* proved so unremunerative, Schlesinger one day ordered me to work out a method for the *Cornet à pistons*. When I told him about my embarrassment, in not knowing how to deal with the subject, he replied by sending me five different published 'Methods' for the *Cornet à pistons*, at that time the favorite amateur instrument among the younger male population of Paris. I had merely to devise a new sixth method out of these five, as all Schlesinger wanted was to publish an edition of his own. I was racking my brains how to start, when Schlesinger, who had just obtained a new complete method, released me from the onerous task. I was, however, told to write fourteen 'Suites' for the *Cornet à pistons*—that is to say, arias out of operas arranged for this instrument. To furnish me with material for this work, Schlesinger sent me no less than sixty complete operas arranged for the piano. I looked them through for suitable arias for my 'Suites,' marked the pages in the volumes with paper strips, and arranged them into a curious looking structure around my work table, so that I might have the greatest possible variety of the melodic material within my reach. When I was in the midst of this work, however, to my great relief and to my poor wife's consternation, Schlesinger told me that M. Schlitz, the first cornet player in Paris, who had looked my 'Etudes' through, preparatory to their being engraved, had declared that I knew absolutely nothing about the instrument, and had generally adopted keys that were too high, which Parisians would never be able to use. The part of the work I had already done was, however, accepted, Schlitz having agreed to correct it, but on the condition that I should share my fee with him.[10]

10 Ibid., 229.

In one of the newspaper articles he wrote at this very time ('The Opera Lies Dying,' written February 23, 1841, for the Dresden *Abendzeitung*), Wagner praises a set of variations by Vieuxtemps and compares it with the kind of popular variations he was working on for Schlesinger.

> At last someone has dared boldly to step forth from the endless row of applause seeking virtuosos with their dreadful airs varies, and restore his art to its proper position of dignity! Somebody has dared to stand up in front of the crowd and fill their pampered ears with the sound of a pure and noble composition.

In an autobiographical note written the following year (1842) Wagner gives a slightly different account of this episode. Here he indicated the *Rienzi* was finished and that he made arrangements for Schlesinger not only of material for the cornet, but for 'all the instruments under heaven.'[11]

Still another version, written nine years later, in 1851, suggests that he was willing to work on even lower musical projects and that the cornet work might have been in fact a 'step up.'

> Owing to the complete failure of all my other efforts, financial straits at last compelled me to a still deeper degradation of the character of my artistic activity. I declared my willingness to concoct the music for a slangy *vaudeville* at a Boulevard theater. But even this step was frustrated by the jealousy of a musical money grubber. So I had to look on it almost as my salvation, that I obtained the chance of doing violence to myself with the arrangement of melodies from 'favorite' operas for the cornet à pistons.[12]

Perhaps the most honest passage of all is one found in an article, written in 1841 for Dresden, in which Wagner describes an evening at the Paris Opera for his German readers. We can surely recognize, in a passage describing various members of the public present, this picture of himself:

> Do you see that young musician there, with pale cheeks and a devouring look in the eyes? With breathless haste he listens to the performance, gulps down the outcome of each single number: is it enthusiasm, or jealousy? Ah, it is the care for daily bread, for if the new opera proves a success, he has reason to hope that the publisher will give him orders for 'fantasias' and 'airs varies' on its 'favorite melodies.'[13]

By 1860 Wagner had sufficient reputation that he could fire a careless cornet player from the orchestra in Paris, without difficulties.[14] On the other hand, a player whom Wagner names as being more effective, was Mr. Bar, a cornet player of the Zurich Orchestra,

> whom I appointed leader of the brass section, as he exercised a great influence on that part of the orchestra. I cannot remember ever having heard the long, powerful chords of the last movement of the C minor Symphony [of Beethoven] executed with such intense power as by this player in Zurich.[15]

[11] 'Autobiographic Sketch,' in Wagner, *Richard Wagner's Prose Works*, 1:18.

[12] 'A Communication to my Friends,' in ibid., 1:303.

[13] 'Halévy's *Reine de Chypre*,' in ibid., 7:207.

[14] Wagner, *My Life*, 727.

[15] Ibid., 554.

Regarding trumpet music of a completely different type, the ancient aristocratic trumpet choirs of Germany, one might suppose Wagner found little pleasure in this style, as he refers to the court, 'where gold laced trumpeters had blown the banal fanfare.'[16] However, Wagner had his own aristocratic bent, as everyone knows, and so it is no surprise to find him employing his own trumpet in this old style.

> Once again I invited all my faithful singers and musicians to assemble in my garden for a farewell party; everywhere was illuminated, as it had been for my last birthday; the children had arranged another torchlight procession. I then bade the trumpeter call my guests together.[17]

Finally, an extant poster, placed outside the Bayreuth Theater in 1876, reads, 'The beginning of each act will be announced by a call of trumpets [Trompeten-Signal], upon which the seats should be taken at once.' We presume this trumpet fanfare was one of those written by Wagner for the local militia.[18]

The Horn

In his essay on conducting, Wagner speaks of his attempts to refine the orchestra's concept of Weber's *Freischütz Overture* in a performance in Vienna and pays tribute to the principal horn.

> Under the refined artistic lead of R. Lewi, the horns altogether changed their style of attack in the dreamy forest-fantasie of the introduction. Instead of braying it out like a swaggering piece of claptrap, they brought it into keeping with the pianissimo of the strings, as prescribed by the score, thus giving the melody an intended witching fragrance.[19]

On another occasion Wagner, homesick in Paris, says he knows his countrymen will understand that upon hearing a performance of *Der Freischütz* at the Paris Opera, he wept on hearing 'from the distance, the blithe dance music of the horns.'[20] Some years later in Paris he experienced great frustration in finding horns who could perform well the music of *Tannhäuser*. His account of this is particularly interesting because he also mentions Adolph Sax, in a phrase which suggests he could have told us a great deal more.

[16] 'Bayreuth (The Playhouse),' in Wagner, *Richard Wagner's Prose Works*, 5:331.

[17] Letter to King Ludwig II, August 22, 1875.

[18] These trumpet fanfares are available from <www.whitwellbooks.com>.

[19] 'About Conducting,' in Wagner, *Richard Wagner's Prose Works*, 4:326.

[20] 'Le Freischutz,' in ibid., 7:184.

It was impossible in the whole of Paris to find the twelve French horns which in Dresden had so bravely sounded the hunting call in the first act. In connection with this matter I had to deal with the terrible man Sax, the celebrated instrument maker. He had to help me out with all kinds of substitutes in the shape of saxophones and saxhorns, moreover he was officially appointed to conduct the music behind the scenes. It was an impossibility ever to get this music properly played.[21]

In recalling a performance of Spohr's *Jessonda*, which he heard in Leipzig, Wagner comments on the principal point of discussion by all composers during the middle nineteenth century—the opposing natures of the natural and valved horn.

The horn's first solo was blown too loud, and with a perceptible taint of affectation—in which I recognized the failing common to all our hornists since the invention of the valve horn.[22]

In 1859, when Wagner was living in Switzerland and was finishing his *Tristan*, he writes of having enjoyed heard, 'Two good horn players who gave me great pleasure by providing a performance of simple folksongs almost regularly in a boat on the lake.'[23]

In his fictional account of a humble German composer's 'Pilgrimage to Beethoven,' there is a disgusting character who tags along, an English amateur who 'plays flute twice a week, horn on Thursday, and composes on Sunday.' The composer says at one point, 'That terrible scale on the horn in the Englishman's hotel filled me with so overpowering a weariness of life, that I there and then resolved to die.'

This story also mentions at one point 'the postilion blew his horn,' a reference to the signal horn of the public, or mail, coach, an institution which is memorialized in Mahler's *Third Symphony*. A sequel, written in 1841, describes the composer and the narrator enjoying a pleasant conversation before an outdoor evening concert, during which they found that, among other things, 'We were agreed that nothing is more prosaic and upsetting than the hideous aspect of the swollen cheeks and puckered features of the wind players.'[24]

[21] Wagner, *My Life*, 761.

[22] 'Spohr's *Jessonda* at Leipzig,' in Wagner, *Richard Wagner's Prose Works*, 6:6.

[23] Wagner, *My Life*, 711.

[24] 'A Pilgrimage to Beethoven,' in Wagner, *Richard Wagner's Prose Works*, 7:26 and 'An End in Paris,' in 7:65, and 70.

The Trombone

During the visit of Spontini to Dresden for the production of his *Vestale*, Wagner asked the visiting composer, in view of the fact that he had made lavish use of trombones in the rest of his scores, why had he not used them in the Triumphal March in the first act of this opera? Spontini answered, 'Are there no trombones there?' Wagner said no and showed him the published score, in which the publisher had apparently omitted them. Spontini begged Wagner to add them before the next rehearsal. In addition, Spontini asked if Wagner would also write a part for the tuba, an instrument Spontini had noticed in the score for *Rienzi* and claimed not to know. While this is highly unlikely, the tuba having been invented in Berlin by a friend of Spontini, nevertheless Wagner says he did this.

> I was delighted to carry out his wish, with moderation and discretion. When he heard the effect for the first time, at rehearsal, he threw me a truly tender glance of thanks, and the impression made on him by this not very difficult enrichment of his score was so lasting that he sent me afterwards a most friendly letter from Paris, begging me to forward him a copy of this instrumental addition; only, his pride did not allow him to admit, in the expression used to signify his wish, that he was asking for anything from my own pen, so he wrote, 'Send me the score for trombones and tuba which were performed under my direction in Dresden.'[25]

[25] 'Mementoes of Spontini,' in ibid., 3:133.

Another charming story Wagner tells is of an occasion when Liszt was asked by a German prince, who was an amateur composer of operas, if the latter could obtain the aid of Wagner in the instrumentation of his work. In particular, the prince wanted some 'trombone effects' similar to those in *Tannhäuser*. Liszt apparently found a way to 'divulge the secret' to the prince that one has to first have a musical idea before it can be set to instruments. Wagner says its true, 'I can never compose when nothing occurs to me.'[26]

[26] 'On Operatic Poetry and Composition,' in ibid., 6:169.

The Tuba

There is an interesting notice regarding the tuba in an extended memorandum on the state of the Dresden orchestra, which Wagner wrote in 1846. In this document Wagner mentions that one of the string bass players was required to double on the tuba. Wagner recommends a raise of 50 talers per year for this overworked man, 'because he has to play two instruments and needs the best nourishment possible to give him the strength.'[27]

It should also be mentioned that the so-called 'Wagnerian tuba' had not been developed by the time of the first Ring performances in Vienna and these parts were played by tuba players from a military band.[28] One of the copyists engaged for making parts at this time was Brahms!

The Percussion Instruments

In an autobiographical sketch, written in 1842 at the request of his friend, Heinrich Laube, for publication the following year in a journal called *Zeitung für die Elegante Welt*, Wagner recalled the very first performance of one of his youthful compositions and its employment of the bass drum.

> My liking for study dwindled more and more, and I chose instead to write Overtures for full orchestra—one of which was once performed in the Leipzig Theater. For its better understanding by whomever might care to study this score, I elected to employ for its notation three separate colors of ink: red for strings, green for woodwinds, and black for the brass. Beethoven's Ninth Symphony was a mere Pleyel Sonata by the side of this marvelously concocted Overture.
>
> Its performance was mainly distinguished by a fortissimo thud on the big drum, which recurred throughout the whole overture at regular intervals of four bars, with the result that the audience gradually passed from its initial amazement at the obstinacy of the bass drummer to undisguised displeasure, and finally to a mirthful mood that much disquieted me.[29]

After the first performance of his early opera, *Liebesverbot*, in Magdeburg, in 1836, Wagner mentions that a well-meaning Prussian military band director 'who felt it his duty to give me a well-meant hint on the handling of the Turkish drum [bass drum] in future operas.[30] There is a moment in this opera

[27] Curt von Westernhagen, *Wagner* (Cambridge: Cambridge University Press, 1978), 1:90.

[28] Ibid., 308–309.

[29] 'Autobiographic Sketch,' in Wagner, *Richard Wagner's Prose Works*, 1:6.

[30] 'Das Liebesverbot,' in ibid., 7:10.

when after 'a roll of the drums,' the chief constable *Brighella* reads out the edict of the city, reminding one of the traditional medieval use of the civic herald to have either percussion or a trumpet play to collect an audience to hear his official announcement.

By his maturity, we can see that Wagner had developed considerable expertise for percussion instruments. Consider, for example, a letter specifying instruments needed for a forthcoming production of *Parsifal* in London in 1881.

> I am now making preparations for the production of Parsifal. Having fared so badly with our English dragon, let us see if we cannot do any better with the Grail *bells*.
>
> Following a discussion with experts on the best way of representing the necessary sound, we agreed after all that it could best be imitated by means of *Chinese tamtams*. In what market are these tamtams to be found in the greatest number and best selection? It is thought to be London. Good! Who will be responsible for selecting them? Dannreuther, of course. And so, my dearest friend, try to track down 4 tamtams which will produce—at least an approximation of—the following peal [C, G, A, and E in bass clef]. It should be noted that—in order to produce a deep bell-like sound—these instruments must be struck only *gently* near the rim, whereas if you hit them sharply in the middle they produce a much brighter sound that is quite unusable.[31]

Wagner's acute attention to all performance details resulted in one criticism when he thought the percussion was playing too loud,

> The drummer apparently thought he was beating his ill-behaved children, for not having brought him his supper from town.[32]

[31] Letter to Edward Dannreuther, April 1, 1881.

[32] 'A Happy Evening,' in Wagner, *Richard Wagner's Prose Works*, 7:75.

Part 4

On Bands and their Music

On Bands and their Music

WAGNER'S INTRODUCTION to the world of music, as a listener, came as a boy when he heard military bands playing in the streets. Musically and aesthetically it formed a bad impression of bands which stayed with him until late in life. Once in discussing the urgent need for schools to teach authentic performance practice in the works of the earlier masters, he confessed,

> I, too, have been to no school for [performance practice], but I reaped a negative lesson as to the proper interpretation for our great works of music from my deep and growing disgust at the performances I heard of our great music, whether at high school concerts or on the military parade ground.[1]

He had a very bad image of band conductors as well and he comments on them frequently in his various publications. A typical example reads,

> In the little theater at *Würzburg* I chanced upon a performance of *Don Juan* ... [in which] a worthy time-beater at the conductor's desk seemed trying to show what his singers could do with even a tempo incorrect throughout. I learned that the Director had imported this person from Temesvar, after enticing him from a military band with whom he used to arrange very popular garden concerts.[2]

In a letter to Robert Schumann, Wagner complains about the aesthetic problem familiar to band concerts in which serious aesthetic works are mixed with popular music. He only admits that for the sake of the audience it is probably better than if they were out drinking:

> We have nothing here to compare with your Gewandhaus concerts, and the only wretched substitute we have to offer are the subscription concerts organized by the director of music of a military band, although it must be said that these concerts are accorded a degree of interest on the part of our audiences which might well find a more worthy outlet elsewhere.[3]

[1] 'Introduction to the Bayreuther Blätter,' in Richard Wagner, *Richard Wagner's Prose Works*, trans., William Ashton Ellis (New York: Broude Brothers, 1966), 6:24.

[2] 'The German Opera Stage of Today,' in ibid., 5:264.

[3] John N. Burk, *Letters of Richard Wagner* (New York: Vienna House, 1972), 104. This in fact was how the famous British brass band movement began, with mill owners worried about their workers getting drunk after work.

In a later time Wagner was still raging over hearing in a concert hall the music of Beethoven juxtaposed with excerpts of Rossini operas and gallops.[4] In an autobiographical story he recalled how insulted he was when a publisher suggested he first needed to make his name by composing 'gallops and pot-pourris.'[5]

As mentioned above, Wagner's introduction to bands came in the market place, the source of all public entertainment in the small German village of the nineteenth century. In his autobiography, he speaks of the wonders seen there during his childhood in Eisleben, acrobats, men who walked on ropes high above the square, and especially a band.

> The thing that attracted me most, however, was the brass band of a Hussar regiment quartered at Eisleben. It often played a certain piece which had just come out, and which was making a great sensation. I mean the 'Huntsmen's Chorus' from Freischütz, that had been recently performed at the Opera in Berlin.[6]

Another significant impression of his youth was a visit to Prague. It is interesting that he came in contact there with an important family in the history of the wind band, that of Count Pachta. It was an earlier Count Pachta who established the real *Harmoniemusik* tradition of the Classical Period and there remain today in the National Library in Prague many such works which belonged to his library. While the present Count Pachta no longer employed a *Harmoniemusik*, one may assume he was also an important figure in Prague art circles. Wagner returned to his estates in Provonin several years later, 1832, for a five-week vacation.[7]

Wagner's first theater position was with a small company in Magdeburg, where the town band, as doublers, became the theater orchestra.[8] When he needed additional players he turned to a Prussian regimental band stationed nearby.[9]

At this early stage in Wagner's career we can assume that his personal exposure to military bands was of a world of functional and entertainment music, something far removed from the aspirations of the young opera composer. One can understand, therefore, how despondent he was when a court author-

[4] 'The Virtuoso and the Artist,' in Wagner, *Richard Wagner's Prose Works* 7:113.

[5] 'A Pilgrimage to Beethoven,' in ibid., 7:23.

[6] Richard Wagner, *My Life* (New York: Tudor, 1911), 7.

[7] Letter to Theodor Apel, December 16, 1832.

[8] Wagner, *My Life*, 106.

[9] Ibid., 135.

ity in Berlin recommended he transcribe some music from his *Tannhäuser* for military band as a means of bringing the music to the notice of the king.

> The consequences of my earlier blindness as to my true position toward the public now made themselves appallingly evident: the impossibility of procuring *Tannhäuser* a popular success, or even a circulation among the German theaters was clear as day. Therewith I was confronted with the complete downfall of my outer circumstances. Almost solely to stave off that downfall, I still made further efforts to spread this opera; and, with that end in view, I turned towards Berlin. By the Intendant of the Royal Prussian State I was waved aside with the critical verdict that my opera was too 'epically' constructed to be suitable for production in Berlin.
>
> The General-Intendant of the Royal Prussian Court music however, appeared to be of another opinion. When, in order to gain the royal interest for the production of my work, I begged him to induce the King to allow me to dedicate *Tannhäuser* to his Majesty, I received for reply the advice that—seeing, on the one hand, the King only accepted works which were already known to him, but on the other, there were obstacles in the way of producing this opera upon the Berlin Court stage—I had better assist His Majesty to an acquaintance with the work in question by arranging something from it for a military band, which something could then be played before the King during the 'change of guard.' I could scarcely have been more deeply humbled, nor brought to a more precise knowledge of my situation![10]

[10] 'A Communication to my Friends,' in Wagner, *Richard Wagner's Prose Works*, 1:339.

The association of military bands, orchestras and opera was a close one throughout Germany during the first half of the nineteenth century. Because of the popularity of military bands they were often added as a stage device in operas. Wagner, himself, had included a cavalry band, consisting of 6 valve and 6 natural trumpets, 6 trombones, 4 ophicleides, and 8 drums in his *Rienzi*. Wagner considered this an important subject, as we can see in a letter of 1842 which he wrote to a court official.

> I am not ready to forfeit a single detail of the musical pomp on the stage; it is absolutely necessary and can easily be managed with the help of the military and other musical bands—certainly my requirements are not the usual ones—I demand an extraordinary band, not put together like the ordinary band … See to it that the trumpeters and trombonists accompanying the warlike cortege of Colonna and Orsini in the first act are chosen from the cavalry and appear on horses … in operas like mine, it must be all or nothing.[11]

[11] Wagner made similar comments in a letter to the Dresden actor, Ferdinand Heine in 1842.

In his essay, 'On the Performing of "Tannhäuser",' Wagner gives additional commentary on the use of stage bands in opera.

> For the musical equipment of the stage itself I have made still more unwonted demands. If I stand by the exactest observance of my instructions for the stage-music, I am justified by the knowledge that in all the more important cities of Germany there exist large and well-manned music-corps, especially belonging to the military, and from these the stage-music-corps required for 'Tannhäuser' can readily be combined.
>
> …
>
> I further urge the regisseur to guard against the processions in 'Tannhäuser' being carried out by the stage personnel in the manner of the customary March, now stereotyped in all our operatic productions. Marches, in the ordinary sense, are not to be found in my later operas; therefore if the entry of the guests into the Singers' Hall (Act II, Scene 4) be so effected that the choir and supers march upon the stage in double file, draw the favorite serpentine curve around it, and take possession of the winds like two regiments of well-drilled troops, in wait for further operatic business—then I merely beg the band to play some march from 'Norma' or 'Belisario,' but not my music. If on the contrary one thinks it as well to retain my music, the entry of the guests must be so ordered as to thoroughly imitate real life, in its noblest, freest forms. Away with that painful regularity of the traditional marching order![12]

12 'The Performing of *Tannhäuser*,' in Wagner, *Richard Wagner's Prose Works*, 3:191, 193.

Finally, in the same spirit, when Wagner added a military band to the orchestra for the ending of his *Rule Britannia Overture*, he was only doing what was seen on the stage everywhere.

On the other hand, none of the bands and none of the band music Wagner had ever heard would have prepared him for the band music he heard in Paris in 1840—The Berlioz *Symphony for Band*, in its first outdoor performance! Wagner was quite taken by this work, which is all the more interesting to the modern reader because there is every evidence that he was not particularly impressed with some of the other Berlioz compositions which today are considered greater masterpieces.

In his autobiography, written much later when Berlioz's reputation was established beyond doubt, Wagner 'edited' his memory to make his early judgment less striking. For example, in the autobiography he mentions the *Romeo and Juliet* with rather some criticism, but also with careful praise.

At first the grandeur and masterly execution of the orchestral part almost overwhelmed me. It was beyond anything I could have conceived. The fantastic daring, the sharp precision with which the boldest combinations—almost tangible in their clearness—impressed me, drove back my own ideas of the poetry of music with brutal violence into the very depths of my soul. I was simply all ears for things of which till then I had never dreamt, and which I felt I must try to realize. True, I found a great deal that was empty and shallow in his *Romeo and Juliet*, a work that lost much by its length and form of combination; and this was the more painful to me seeing that, on the other hand, I felt overpowered by many really bewitching passages which quite overcame any objections on my part.[13]

> [13] Wagner, *My Life*, 234.

On the other hand, the descriptions he actually wrote at the time, on hearing *Romeo and Juliet*, have a different flavor and suggest far less enthusiasm.

In this work there are so many examples of tastelessness and so many artistic blemishes, ranged side by side with passages of pure genius, that I could not help wishing that Berlioz had shown it before the performance to a man like Cherubini, who would certainly have known how to remove a large number of its ugly distortions without in any way harming the original as a whole.[14]

> [14] Report to the Dresden *Abendzeitung*, May 5, 1841.

Similarly, in a letter written at this time, Wagner observes,

The first piece of his that I heard was his Romeo & Juliet symphony, in which the insipidity of the work's outward economy violently repelled me, for all the composer's evident genius.[15]

> [15] Letter to Ferdinand Heine, March 27, 1841.

This tone is maintained in a brief autobiographical sketch to the year 1842.

Despite his stand-off manners, Berlioz attracted me in a far higher degree. He differs by the whole breadth of heaven from his Parisian colleagues, for he makes no music for gold. But he cannot write for the sake of purest art; he lacks all sense of beauty. He stands, completely isolated, upon his own position; by his side he has nothing but a troupe of devotees who, shallow and without the smallest spark of judgment, greet in him the creator of a brand new musical system and completely turn his head—the rest of the world avoids him as a madman.[16]

> [16] 'Autobiographical sketch,' in Wagner, *Richard Wagner's Prose Works*, 1:15.

With this background, and with our knowledge that he also previously knew *both* the *Harold in Italy* and the *Symphonie Fantastique*, the reader will appreciate how extraordinary indeed is his praise for the Berlioz *Symphony for Band*. In his autobiography, Wagner recalls,

> It was, however, the latest work of this wonderful master, his *Trauer-Symphonie für die Opfer der Juli-Revolution*, most skillfully composed for massed military bands during the summer of 1840 for the anniversary of the obsequies of the July heroes, and conducted by him under the column of the Place de la Bastille, which had at last thoroughly convinced me of the greatness and enterprise of this incomparable artist. But while admiring this genius, absolutely unique in his methods, I could never quite shake off a certain peculiar feeling of anxiety. His works left me with a sensation as of something strange, something with which I felt I should never be able to be familiar, and I was often puzzled at the strange fact that, though ravished by his compositions, I was at the same time repelled and even wearied by them. It was only much later that I succeeded in clearly grasping and solving this problem, which for years exercised such a painful spell over me.
>
> It is a fact that at this time I felt almost like a little schoolboy by the side of Berlioz.[17]

[17] Wagner, *My Life*, 235.

The account Berlioz wrote at the time, for the Dresden *Abendzeitung*, is no less enthusiastic and once again sets the band symphony above the other major works of Berlioz in quality.

> His virtue is that he does not write for money, and anybody who knows Paris and the ways of French composers will appreciate the value of this virtue in this country. Berlioz is a sworn enemy of everything vulgar, beggarly or commercial. He has vowed to strangle the first organ-grinder who dares to play any of his tunes … All the same, it cannot be denied that Berlioz is well able to write a truly popular composition, although here I use the word 'popular' in its most ideal sense. When I heard his symphony written to commemorate the reburial of the victims of the July Revolution I had the vivid feeling that every street-urchin in blue shirt and red cap must have understood it down to the very last note. Of course I should feel inclined to call it a national rather than a popular understanding, for it is quite a long step from *Le Postillon de Longjumeau* to this July Symphony. But truly I feel tempted to give this work of Berlioz's precedence over all the others. It is big and noble from beginning to end: what it may contain of morbid exaltation is checked and overridden by a patriotic enthusiasm raising the lament to the lofty peak of its final apotheosis. When I furthermore place to Berlioz's credit the noble treatment of the military band instruments, which

were all he had at his disposal, then I must take back—at least as far as this symphony is concerned—what I previously said about the likely fate of Berlioz's compositions: I gladly predict that this July Symphony will continue to live and provide inspiration as long as a nation that calls itself France exists.[18]

[18] 'Letters from Paris, 1841,' in Wagner, *Richard Wagner's Prose Works*, 8:135.

Wagner praised the final movement of this band composition again the following year in a letter to Robert Schumann.

Not long ago he gave a concert which systematically drove people insane. Those who had not already been driven mad with boredom and *degout* certainly had been by the end of the apotheosis of his July Symphony—but out of *joy*; that is the remarkable thing: in this last movement there are passages so magnificent and sublime that they can *never* be surpassed.[19]

[19] Letter to Robert Schumann, February 5, 1842.

And in a passing comment that 'each of Berlioz's Symphonies reveals the inner necessity from which the composer could not tear himself.'[20]

What did Wagner think when he heard bands play transcriptions of his own music? There are several such accounts and they vary considerably in the circumstances they describe. In his autobiography he describes an evening serenade on Lake Lucerne during the Summer of 1856, an occasion which he remembered more for the fellowship than the music.

[20] 'Der Freischütz,' in Wagner, *Richard Wagner's Prose Works*, 7:178.

Two boats, illuminated by colored lanterns, came up to the beach facing our hotel, bearing the Brunnen brass band, which was formed entirely of amateurs from the countryside. With Federal staunchness, and without any attempts at punctilious unison, they proceeded to play some of my compositions in a loud and irrefutable manner. They then paid me homage in a little speech, and I replied heartily, after which there was much gripping of all sorts of horny hands on my part, as we drank a few bottles of wine on the beach. For years afterward I never passed this beach … without receiving a friendly handshake or a greeting.[21]

[21] Wagner, *My Life*, 647ff.

In other accounts, Wagner seems to have enjoyed these opportunities on a musical level. There is no question that when he heard a fine military band at mid-century, he would be hearing a level of performance which, in many ways, would surpass theater orchestras in all but the largest cities. Certainly, this must have been the case with the Austrian band he heard in Venice during the Winter of 1858–1859.

Strangely enough, it was the thoroughly German element of good military music, to which so much attention is paid in the Austrian army, that brought me into touch with public life in Venice. The conductors in the two Austrian regiments quartered there began playing overtures of mine, *Rienzi* and *Tannhäuser* for instance, and invited me to attend their rehearsals in their barracks. There I also met the whole staff of officers, and was treated by them with great respect. These bands played on alternate evenings amid brilliant illuminations in the middle of the Piazza San Marco, whose acoustic properties for this class of production were really excellent. I was often suddenly startled towards the end of my meal by the sound of my own overtures; then, as I sat at the restaurant window giving myself up to impressions of the music, I did not know which dazzled me most, the incomparable piazza magnificently illuminated and filled with countless numbers of moving people, or the music that seemed to be borne away in rustling glory to the winds. Only one thing was missing that might certainly have been expected from an Italian audience: the people were gathered around the band in thousands listening most intently, but no two hands ever forgot themselves so far as to applaud, as the least sign of approbation of Austrian military music would have been looked upon as treason to the Italian Fatherland.[22]

[22] Ibid., 696.

A letter Wagner wrote at this time (24 October 1858) thanking one of these Austrian conductors reveals, more than the passage from his autobiography quoted above, his genuine appreciation.

> Honorable Conductor,
>
> I could not find you in the Piazza yesterday to thank you for the wonderful performance of the *Rienzi Overture*, so today I do this in this written form. I appreciated it very much that your musicians had noticed everything, had marked everything so well and brought everything out correctly. From the very beginning it was perfect, with the tempo entirely correct. [My only suggestion is that] four bars before the Allegro there should be more drums and very strong; that place is dull.
>
> Once again, the best thanks and the assurance that you have made it very enjoyable for me.
>
> Auf Wiedersehen!
>
> Yours faithfully,
> Richard Wagner

There is one letter of Wagner, written to Count Redern in Berlin, dated 26 June 1846, which clearly establishes the fact that Wagner did not object, in principle, to his music being transcribed for bands.

While I doubt that there are many pieces in my opera that are suitable for production as military music, I permit myself to draw your attention, however, particularly to one number which has gone exceedingly well on parades here in Dresden; I refer to the first section of the fourth scene of the second Act; it is a kind of March ... that lends itself well to treatment as an effective piece for military band. If now a pendant to this is required, perhaps the Pilgrim's Chorus ... could be chosen.

In addition, there is some evidence, given below, that Wagner approved of the transcription of music of the Ring for band.

It could not have escaped Wagner's notice that, because of the popularity of bands in general in Germany, composers, including Liszt, Meyerbeer, and Spontini, sometimes had their music transcribed for bands as a means of introducing the music to the broad public in order to build support for the eventual publication and performance of the original versions. Indeed, remarkable as it may seem, part of *Lohengrin* was performed by a military band in Berlin *before* the premiere of the opera itself by Liszt and the Weimar Court Opera in 1850.[23]

[23] Gottfried Veit, *Die Blasmusik* (Innsbruck: Helbling Edition, 1972), 54.

Towards the end of his life, when he began to be more widely recognized, he must have frequently heard bands playing in his honor in official ceremonies of greeting. A typical case he recalls occurred during his visit to Budapest in 1863.

The Count [Bethlen-Gabor] invited me to a performance by the military bands in the castle at Ofen, where I was graciously received by him and his family, treated to ice cream, and then conducted to a balcony where I listened to a concert given by the massed bands. The effect of all these demonstrations was exceedingly refreshing.[25]

[25] Wagner, *My Life*, 869ff.

In his correspondence Wagner mentions a similar occasion in 1872.

I visited the Grand Duke of Baden ... The [Wagner] Societies of Darmstadt and Mainz have surprised and delighted me, and there was no lack of regimental music in the streets.[26]

[26] Letter to Friedrich Feustel, November 29, 1872.

We know from Wagner's essays relating to the broad question of interpretation that his first concern was always 'the correct tempo.' He always leaves the impression that the poor conductors arrived at their interpretation on the basis of what they had heard and not on the basis of their own score study.[27]

[27] For band conductors today it is from listening to recordings.

Therefore, when he was serenaded by military bands who honored him with renditions of his music in incorrect tempi, Wagner was both displeased and curious on how their interpretations evolved.

Of late I have often been honored by military bands with a very friendly serenade of pieces from my operas. [While] sincerely delighted and truly touched by their doings, for the most part, I have not been able to conceal from their excellent conductors my difficulty in accounting for certain omissions and faulty tempi which I had uniformly noticed in the first finale of 'Lohengrin,' as an example. I was told that they had based their arrangements on the reputedly authoritative score of the Dresden Court Theater, where these passages were missing, and also that one heard this tempo and no other at all the theaters. Whoever has once arrived at hearing the closing Allegro of the first 'Lohengrin' finale played properly in its entirely, may imagine my feelings at listening to the galloping stump of a composition which I had labored to make grow up before me like a well-formed tree, with branches, boughs and leafworks! When I explained this to the highly obliging, and for the most part excellent Kapellmeisters of those bands, they were utterly surprised and often disconcerted. 'How were we to know any better? Indeed we nowhere hear it otherwise' was their invariable reply.[28]

...

I have reaped a negative lesson as to the proper rendering for our great works of music from my deep and growing disgust at the performances I have heard of our great music, whether at high school concerts or on the military parade.[29]

...

We have neither a well nor badly conducted orchestra, at most a regimental band whose renderings show us how Herr Upper-Court-Kapellmeister at the royal seat is minded as to tempo and that sort of thing.[30]

The diaries of his wife, Cosima, also contain complaints on hearing her husband's music with incorrect tempi.

They're beginning—a military band—Tannhäuser overture; poor, poor Meister, everywhere the same torment, the same wrong tempi.

...

My God! they won't stop, now they're playing the Soldiers' Chorus from Faust. You see, 'more appetite than taste,' my head is reeling![31]

[28] 'The German Opera Stage of Today,' in Wagner, *Richard Wagner's Prose Works*, 5:278.

[29] 'Introduction to Bayreuther Blatter,' in ibid., 6:24.

[30] Ibid., 6:26.

[31] Curt von Westernhagen, *Wagner* (Cambridge: Cambridge University Press), 2:453.

Finally, a military band met the train which brought the body of the late composer to Bayreuth and several bands performed funeral dirges as the procession moved through the city toward his home, Wahnfried.[32]

32 Henry T. Finck, *Richard Wagner and his Works* (New York: Greenwood Press, 1968), 2:453.

Part 5

On the Music for Band

Festgesang, 'Der Tag erscheint,' (Weihegruss)

COMPOSED:
May 1843, for TTBB, 4 horns, 4 trumpets, 3 trombones,
and tuba

SOURCE:
Private Collection: full score

PUBLICATION:
Samtliche Werke (Mainz, 1970), 16

FIRST PERFORMANCE:
7 June 1843, Dresden

The account which Wagner left of this composition, while
rich in some details unfortunately is not clear with regard to
the instrumentation used at the first performance. Was it an
unaccompanied vocal work or one with brass instruments.
Both versions survive in early sources.

On the 7th of June of this year (1843) the statue of King Frederick
Augustus by Rietschl was unveiled in the Dresden Zwinger with all due
pomp and ceremony. In honor of this event I, in collaboration with
Mendelssohn, was commanded to compose a festival song and to conduct the gala performance. I had written a simple song for male voices
of modest design, whereas to Mendelssohn had been assigned the more
complicated task of interweaving the National Anthem into the male
chorus he had to compose. This he had effected by an artistic work in
counterpoint, so arranged that from the first eight beats of his original
melody the brass instruments simultaneously played the Anglo-Saxon
popular air. My simpler song seems to have sounded very well from a
distance, whereas I understood that Mendelssohn's daring combination
quite missed its effect, because no one could understand why the vocalists did not sing the same tune that the wind instruments were playing.[1]

[1] Richard Wagner, *My Life* (New York: Tudor, 1911), 312.

In a letter written at this time to his brother, Albert, Wagner
gives essentially the same information.

On the 7th we had a grand festivity here, the unveiling of the monument to Friedrich August. A chant for men's voices—to be executed in the Zwinger—was ordered of me by the King. Mendelssohn had to compose the second one. My chorus, being simple, uplifting and effective, decidedly bore off the palm; whereas Mendelssohn's turned out both pompous and flat. The King sent me best thanks and a beautiful gold snuffbox worth about 100 thaler.

Another letter, of 13 July 1843, which Wagner wrote to his half-sister, Cacilie, gives us the size of the choral forces.

Reissiger went off on holiday in the middle of May, leaving me practically on my own to carry out all the duties, both in church & in the theater, in addition to which I received a commission from the King to write a commemorative hymn for the unveiling of the memorial to King Friedrich August. Mendelssohn was also commissioned to write a piece. The overall control of the performance, which took place in the Zwinger, was entrusted to me. I assembled a choir of 250 singers from the local choral societies, & made a great name for myself, in that it was universally agreed that my own piece, which was straightforward & uplifting, knocked Mendelssohn's over-elaborate & artificial composition into a cocked hat.

Most books on the music of Wagner assume this festival song was unaccompanied, simply because Wagner mentions no instruments in his account in his autobiography. We know the version for male choir, trumpets, horns, trombones, and tuba which was published in the 'Complete Works,' in 1913.

What, then, was the version sung at the original ceremony? To this writer there is first the matter of circumstance. Both Wagner and Mendelssohn write a work for 250 male singers for the same performance. Brass instruments are available and used for the Mendelssohn work. It does not make much sense that the Wagner version with brass was not also used. The fact that he refers to his music as 'simple,' still describes it, but should not be taken to mean unaccompanied.

The stronger argument is the music itself. This is not a brass accompaniment added later to a preexistent vocal piece. The brass parts here are sometimes independent, with non-harmonic notes not found at all in the vocal parts. Thirty-three bars from the end the brass ensemble has music for itself alone, the singers have a rest. What happened here on 7 June 1843, if the work were sung *a cappella*?

The source of the title 'Weihegruss' is unknown.

Trauermusik (Trauersinfonie)

Composed:
Early November 1844, for large concert band

Sources:
Berlin, Staatsbibliothek zu Berlin Preussicher Kulturbesitz,
  Musikabteiling: full score (dated 18 November 1844!)
Bayreuth-Wahnfried: original piano draft

Publication:
Dresden, 1860 (piano score)
Richard Wagner Werke (Leipzig, 1912–1929), xx, as *Trauersinfonie*
Samtliche Werke (Mainz, 1970), 18/ii (full score)

First Performance:
14 December 1844, Catholic Cemetery, Friedrichstadt (Dresden)

This work is based on the music of, and was created in honor of, Carl Maria von Weber. Weber died in 1826 in London, while on a musical tour, and was buried with great pomp in Moorfields Chapel in Finsbury Circus.

Fifteen years later, on 21 January 1841, an anonymous letter appeared in the *Gazette Musicale* (Paris) which recalled a visit to this crypt with the object of finding the final resting place of Weber. The writer details considerable difficulty in finding the coffin of the composer, even with the help of one of the local sextons. Eventually he finds the coffin, shaped like the body of a violin, in an apparent state of neglect.

The whole tone of this account seems to have had an immediate impact on the musicians in Dresden. By March another notice in the same paper mentions that a subscription drive was in progress in an attempt to raise the necessary funds to bring the remains of Weber home.[1] This effort, in addition to a benefit concert, apparently failed to achieve its goal and the entire project had been temporarily abandoned when Wagner took up the challenge early in 1844. His initial approach to the

[1] Wagner has left a lengthy account of the process in his 'Weber's Re-interment (Report),' in Richard Wagner, *Richard Wagner's Prose Works*, trans., William Ashton Ellis (New York: Broude Brothers, 1966), 7:228ff.

court theater indendant, Lüttichau, brought a typical bureaucratic response, 'Why is so much trouble being made about Weber' and 'What if the widows of all the Kapellmeisters who had died in foreign lands wanted such ceremonies,' etc. In addition the king had religious scruples regarding disturbing the last sleep of death.

The eldest of Weber's two sons went to London and returned with the coffin to Magdeburg on the morning of 14 December 1844. In the evening a boat, draped in black and decorated with poems and lanterns, brought it to the bank of the Elbe.

The coffin was then placed on a magnificent catafalque in the center of a group of some three hundred artists and amateurs, each holding a wax taper and laurel wreath. Then four hundred singers sang a funeral hymn composed by Wagner. Following this, and joined by five hundred soldiers of the royal guard, carrying torches, and procession was made to the Catholic cemetery. The church bells of the city were tolling and the street was illuminated by innumerable candles, placed in the windows along the route. Presumably it was for this procession that the *Trauermusik* was used.[2]

Wagner's own account of this episode, 'Report on the homecoming of the mortal remains of Karl Maria von Weber from London to Dresden,' he published in Volume 2 of his *Complete Writings*.

[2] Adolphe Jullien, *Richard Wagner* (Neptune, NJ: Paganiniana Publications, 1981), 77ff.

> A beautiful and earnest incident reacted on the mood in which I was already finishing the composition of 'Tannhäuser' at the end of the dying year, and profitably neutralized the various distractions rising from my outward intercourse. It was the ultimate conveyance, in December, 1844, of the mortal remains of *Karl Maria von Weber* from London to Dresden. Some years before, a Committee had been formed to agitate for this removal. A traveler had made known the fact that the modest coffin which sheltered Weber's ashes was stowed in such an out-of-the-way corner of St. Paul's church [sic] in London, that it was to be feared it would soon be past discovery. My energetic friend Professor *Lowe* had profited by this news to rouse the Liedertafel, of which he was the passionately active president, to undertake the transference of Weber's remains. The concert of male singers, given for the purpose of raising the necessary funds, had had a relatively great success; folk were pressing for the Theater to follow suit, when an obstinate resistance was encountered in high quarters. The Dresden General-Direction signified to the Committee that the King held religious scruples against the

proposed disturbance of a dead man's rest. One could scarcely credit
the motive alleged, yet could not well contest it; and so the new era
of my appointment as Kapellmeister was made the plea for obtaining
my advocacy of the plan. I assented with great alacrity, and allowed
myself to be placed on the Committee; an artistic authority, the Director of the Cabinet of Antiques, Herr Hofrath *Schulz*, was added to our
number, together with a banker; the agitation was actively commenced
afresh; appeals were issued in all directions; exhaustive plans were
drafted, and above all, numberless meetings took place. But here again
I fell into antagonism with my chief, Herr *von Luttichau*: he certainly
would have gladly forbidden me to have anything to do with the thing,
under pretext of the Royal Will. But he had had a warning not to pick
a quarrel with me after his experience in the summer, when, contrary
to his expectations, the music written by me to celebrate the King's
arrival had found favor with the monarch. As in any case the King's
objection to the undertaking was not so definitely meant, and my chief
could scarcely help seeing that this Royal Will could not have hindered
its prosecution on a private path; whilst on the other hand it would
bring the Court into bad odor if the Royal Theater, to which *Weber* had
once belonged, were to play the sulking enemy,—Herr *von Luttichau*
rather sought by pleasantries to turn me from my intervention, without which, as he argued, the affair would surely never come about. He
represented how invidious it would be, to pay such extravagant honor
to the memory of precisely *Weber*, when the deceased *Morlacchi* had
served the Royal Kapelle so much longer, yet nobody proposed to fetch
his ashes back from Italy. To what consequences might it not lead? He
put the case that *Reissiger* were shortly to die on a trip to the baths; his
widow then might demand, with just as much right as Frau *von Weber*
now, that the body of her husband should be brought home with hymn
and chant. I tried to reassure him on this point; though I didn't succeed
in making clear to him the difference he had overlooked, yet I managed
to convince him that the thing must now pursue its course, especially as
the Berlin Court Theater had already announced a benefit performance
in support of our object. That performance—instigated by *Meyerbeer*, to
whom my committee had addressed itself—took place with a represen-
tation of 'Euryanthe,' and brought us in the handsome contribution of
full 2,000 thalers. Some minor theaters followed; so that the Dresden
Court Theater could not no longer lag behind, and we soon were able
to hand our banker a sufficient sum to defray the expenses of transport
and provide a seemly vault with a suitable tombstone, and still retain a
nucleus for Weber's statue to be erected later. The older of the immortal
master's orphaned sons made the journey himself to London, to bring
back his father's ashes. The body was brought by ship, up the Elbe, to
the Dresden landing, here first to be restored to German soil.

This transference was to take place in the evening, by torchlight and
in solemn train; I had undertaken to provide the mourning music then
to be performed. I compiled it from two motives of 'Euryanthe' that
portion of the overture which represents the spirit vision I made con-

nect with the cavatina of Euryanthe, '*hier dicht am Quell,*'—also quite
unchanged, though transposed to B flat,—and ended with the trans-
figuration of that first motive, as it recurs at the close of the opera. This
quite appropriate symphonic piece I expressly orchestrated for 80 picked
wind instruments, taking particular care only to use their smoothest reg-
isters, however great the volume; in the section taken from the overture
I replaced the tremolo of the violas by twenty stopped trumpets in the
gentlest piano; and even at the rehearsal in the theater the whole thing
struck so deep a chord in our memory of Weber that not only was Frau
Schroder-Devrient—who was present at the time, and at any rate was a
personal friend of Weber's—most profoundly touched, but I could not
help admitting to myself that I never had wrought out anything so completely answering to its aim. No less successful was the music's execution in the open street when the cortege took its way: as the extremely
slow tempo, accentuated by no plain rhythmic landmarks, was bound to
offer peculiar difficulties, I had had the stage completely cleared at the
rehearsal, to gain the necessary room to let the bandsmen march around
me in a circle while they played the piece, already duly practiced. I was
assured by witnesses who watched the cortege passing, from their windows, that the impression of solemnity had been unspeakably sublime.

After we had laid the coffin in the little mortuary chapel of the
Catholic cemetery in the Friedrichstadt, where it was silently and
reverently welcomed by Frau Devrient with a wreath, on the following
morning was carried out its solemn lowering into the vault prepared for
its reception. To myself and the other president of the committee, Herr
Hofrath Schulz, the honor of delivering a funeral oration had been allot-
ted. Quite recently a singularly touching subject had been furnished me
by the death of the lamented master's second son, Alexander von Weber,
shortly before this reinterment. His mother was so terribly shattered by
the unexpected bereavement of this thriving youth that, had our undertaking not already gone too far, we should almost have seen ourselves
compelled to give it up; for in this fresh so awful loss the widow seemed
disposed to recognize the voice of Heaven indignant at the vanity of
wishing to disturb the ashes of one so long deceased. As the public, in
its prevalent temper, had manifested symptoms of a like belief, I held it
my peculiar duty to place this side of our endeavor in its proper light;
and after my successful vindication I was assured on all hands that not a
word of that was heard again.

Herewith I made a strange experience, as it was the first time in my
life that I had ever had to pronounce a ceremonial speech in public.
Since then, whenever I have had to hold forth, I have always spoken *ex
tempore.* This first time, however, if only to give my speech the needful
terseness, I had written it out and learnt it by heart. As the subject and
my setting of it entirely filled my mind, I was so certain of my memory
that I had taken no thought for any kind of artificial aid; thus it came
that I set my brother Albert—who was standing near me at the ceremony—in great alarm for a moment, and he told me afterwards that,
for all his emotion, he had cursed me for not having supplied him with

the manuscript to prompt me. It was this way: on the beginning my speech in clear full tones, for an instant I was so strongly affected by the almost terrifying impression made upon me by my own voice, its timbre and accent, that in an absolute trance I seemed to see myself, exactly as I heard myself, before the breathless, listening crowd; in this projection of myself I fell into a magnetized expectance of the event that was about to pass before me, precisely as if I were not myself the very being who was standing here and had to speak. Not the smallest fright, or even embarrassment, occurred to me; merely, after an appropriate cadence there followed so disproportionately long a pause, that those who saw me standing with my eyes transfixed were puzzled what to make of me. Only my own long silence and the voiceless hush around me, reminded me that here I had not to hearken, but to speak:

Here rest thee then! Here be the unassuming spot that holds for us thy dear loved relics! And had they flaunted there midst vaults of princes, within the proudest minister of a haughty nation, we dared to hope thou'dst rather choose a modest grave in German soil for thy last resting place. For thou wast none of those chill seekers after fame, who own no fatherland, to whom that plot of earth is dearest where ambition finds the rankest soil in which to thrive. Was it a fate that drove thee whither Genius itself must bring itself to market, thou turn'dst thy yearning gaze towards the hearth of home, towards the modest country nook where, seated with thy loving wife, thy heart welled song on song. 'Ah! were I once more with you, dear ones!'— this was the latest sigh, for sure, wherewith thou pass'dst from life.

Wast *thou* so fond a dreamer, then who shall blame us that we felt alike toward *thee*; if, laying thy fair dreams to heart, we nursed the silent wish to have thee back once more in our dear homeland? That *Schwarmerei* of thine: with all the power of sympathy, it made of thee the darling of thy folk! Never has a more *German* musician lived, than thou. Where'er thy genius bore thee, to whatsoever distant realms of floating fancy, it stayed forever linked by thousand tendrils to the German people's heart; that heart with which it wept and laughed, a child believing in the tales and legends told it of its country. Eh! 'twas this childlikeness that led thy manhood's spirit, the guardian angel that preserved it ever chaste and pure; and in that chasteness lay thy individual stamp. As thou maintain'dst that shining virtue ever spotless, thou neededst naught to ponder, naught invent— thou neededst but to feel, and straightaway hadst thou found the font original. Thou kept'st it till thy death, this highest virtue; thou couldst not cast it off or barter it, that fairest heirloom of thy German birth; thou never couldst betray us! And lo!, the Briton may yield thee justice, the Frenchman admiration; but the German alone can *love* thee. His thou art; a beauteous day amid his life, a warm drop of his own blood, a morsel of his heart—and who shall blame us if we wished thine ashes, too, should mingle with his earth, should form a portion of dear German soil?

Upbraid us not, ye men who so misprized the nature of the German, that heart which dotes on what it loves. Was it dotage bade us claim the precious coil of our dear Weber, then was it that same Schwarmerei that makes us so akin to him, the fantasy whence sprang the glorious blossoms of his genius, for whose sweet sake the world admires, and we, we love him.

And so, dear Weber, 'tis love that prompts us to a work of love, when thee—who never sought'st for admiration, but solely love—we snatch from eyes of admiration and bring to arms of love. From out the world, which thou bedazzledst, we lead thee back into thy country, the bosom of thy family! Ask the hero who went out to victory, what most rejoiced him after glorious days upon the field of honor? For sure, the threshold of the father-house, where wife and child await him. And see! we have no need to speak in images: thy wife, thy children wait for thee in very truth. Soon shalt thou feel above this resting place the tread of thy fond wife, who long—so long!—had waited for thy coming back, and now, beside her darling son, weeps hottest love tears for the homecoming friend of her true heart. To the world of the living, she belongs—and thee, become a blessed spirit, no more can she greet thee face to face; but God hath sent an envoy forth to greet thee eye to eye on thy return, to bear thee tidings of thy dear ones' everlasting love. Thy youngest son was chosen for that office, to knit the bond 'twxt living and deceased; an angel of light he hovers now between you, conveying messages of love from each to each.

Where now is death? Where life? Where both join hands in bond so wondrous fair, there is the seed of life eternal. Let us as well, thou dear departed, commingle in that bond! Then shall we know no longer death, no more decay, but only flower time and harvest. The stone that closes on thy earthly shell shall then become for us the desert rock from which the man of might once smote sweet waters; to farthest ages shall it pour a glorious stream of ever quickened, e'er creative life.

Great Fountain of all being, grant that we prove ever mindful, ever worthy of this bond![3]

3 'Weber's Re-interment (Speech),' in Wagner, *Richard Wagner's Prose Works*, 7:235.

I delivered my speech to the end with such fluency that the famous actor *Emil Devrient* assured me that he had been amazingly impressed by the incident, not only as mourner at the most affecting burial, but in particular as dramatic orator. The ceremony ended with the singing of a poem written and composed by myself for male voices, which, notwithstanding its great difficulty, was admirably rendered under the lead of our best opera singers.

Ye favor'd of this hour, uplift your voices,
This hour whose solemn peace ye all attest!
To mind commit what now our heart rejoices,
To words and tones the joy that swells our breast!

No longer mourns the shrouded German Mother,
Our German Earth, bereft of her dear son;
No longer yearns for our beloved brother
Across the sea, in distant Albion:
She's taken him anew into her womb
Whom once she bore in all his tender bloom.
Here, where the tears of grief were dumbly flowing,
Where love with sobs its dearest still requites,
Here was there knit a bond of hope e'er growing
That us to him, the shining one, unites:
Ye fellows of that bond, come journey hither,
Here greet as pilgrims of one faith and race;
Bring here the fairest flowers, that ne'er can wither,
The flowers of lealty to this noble place:
For here rests he, midst faithful hearts and fond,
Who sheds the dew of blessing on our bond.

Herr von Luttichau, who attended this rite, at all events declared to me that he had now been convinced and persuaded of the rightness of the undertaking.

The whole issue of my labors was consoling to my inmost heart; and had anything been lacking to it, the sincerest thanks of *Weber's* widow, whom I visited on my return from the church yard, contributed to scatter every cloud. For me it had a deep significance, that I whom *Weber's* living presence had won so passionately for music in my earliest childhood, and who later had been so sorely stricken by the tidings of his death, in man's estate should now have entered into immediate personal contact with him through this second burial. From the tenor of my intercourse with living masters of the art of composition, and the experiences I made of them, one may judge at what a fount my yearning for familiar commune with the Masters had to brace itself. It was not consoling, to look from *Weber's* grave toward his living followers; ye the hopelessness of that outlook was only with time to come to my full consciousness.[4]

4 See Wagner, *Richard Wagner's Prose Works*, 7:228ff and Wagner, *My Life,* 357ff.

We may assume that Wagner was the one who did most of the organizational work on this ceremony, as his later letters clearly reflect. For example, in a letter to Karl Gaillard, dated 5 June 1845, Wagner writes,

In spite of the decisive repugnance of the Court and the general manager, I effected the moving of *Weber's* remains to Dresden; the funeral, the dignified ceremony is *my* work. Did you read anything about it in the Dresden reports?

Another letter suggests that not all doubters had in fact been silenced.

For the time being I have not been able to get away from Dresden for a single day. I was detained there by the return of Weber's ashes, which I have brought about and which has been duly carried through. Weber rests in our cemetery now; we got his remains on the 14th inst., and buried them on the 15th. The celebration was beautiful and dignified and by my speech at the grave I succeeded in giving it a due and most stirring significance. But it is truly distressing how this and similar occasions bring envy against me and often much embitter my fine position.[5]

[5] Letter to Ernst Benedikt Kietz, December 18, 1844.

While we have no reason to doubt the close relationship Wagner said he had for Weber in his report of the ceremony quoted above, it is nevertheless interesting to observe that after the association he shared in this ceremony he seemed to have taken on Weber's mantel in trying to lift the standards of the Dresden Opera.

Encouraged by the high standards I found here, I have now set about the glorious task of carrying on Weber's work, i.e., helping to emancipate Dresden musically, taking the philistines for a ride, educating the public taste so that audiences learn to appreciate what is noble in art and in that way making Weber's voice heard.[6]

[6] Letter to Karl Gaillard, June 5, 1845.

Editorial and Performance Notes

The modern edition of this work, revised by Erik Leidzen and published in 1949 by Associated Music Publishers, New York, varies in important detail with Wagner's original manuscript score. The following list represents some of the more important of these and which are particularly significant for performance purposes:

1. The meter should be common time, not alle breve.
2. The tempo indication should read 'Adagio,' not 'Andante maestoso.'
3. The fourth beat of bar 6 should contain an A natural, rather than the B♭, in Euphonium, 2nd and 4th horns, tenor saxophone, bassoons, and bass clarinet.
4. Bar 16 should have E♭ above the staff for 1st trombone, G in the staff for 2nd trombone, and F below the staff for 3rd trombone.

5. The fifth bar after Rehearsal Number 2 should have one long slur, replacing portamento, in the upper woodwinds, which includes the first eighth-note of the following bar.

6. At Rehearsal Number 3, there should be no crescendo until the second bar.

7. The eleventh bar after Rehearsal Number 3 should read *pianissimo* in the horns beginning with the sixteenth-note.

8. Five bars before the so-called 'Coda,' a term not found in the original sources, the tuba should have a low B♭ half-note.

9. In the final two bars all the woodwinds should have tied whole-notes. Trombone 2 should read D, D in the next to last bar and low B♭ in the staff in the final bar. Trombone 3 should read low B♭ in the staff in the final two bars. Euphonium should not play the final two bars. Tuba should read low B♭ in the staff for the next to last bar and an octave lower in the final bar.[7]

The discussion of the interpretation of this masterpiece must begin with the question of the repeat sign. The fact that this repeat sign was present already in the very first piano score[8] confirms that Wagner had this in mind in his original conception and that he intended this repeat to be honored. But in American performances it is rarely honored, perhaps because the conductors think they are merely playing the composition twice, followed by a 'coda,' a designation which inexplicably continues to appear in each new publication even though Wagner himself never used that word. The reason why Wagner would never have thought of the final music as a true coda and the reason why he considered the long repeat not arbitrary is because the form itself is the ancient German Bar Form: AAB.

But, strictly speaking, in the case of any long passage of music, one should not just 'play the music twice,' for such a decision ignores the experience of the listener. For example the first time this theme is heard, at bar 17, it is full outgoing optimism. However, when the time comes for this same music to be repeated a great deal of contemplative music has been heard by the listener in addition to a long, ever slowing, ever softer sensitive cadence ending with a *pp* unison pitch. Emotionally, one simply cannot go from this back to the outgoing,

[7] My own modern edition, which corrects these problems, can be found at <http://www.whitwellbooks.com>.

[8] I believe I may have been the first person to identify the original piano score, which had been labeled merely as 'a sketch' in a small bibliothek which existed at one time in Wagner's home, Wanfried, in Bayreuth. At that time all of Wagner's furniture and his extraordinary silk wall coverings were still in place giving one the strongest possible feeling of the presence of the composer. In a recent visit I was horrified to find that the government had taken over the administration of the home, had removed all the furniture and everything which had belonged to Wagner, and repainted the walls to give the appearance of some modern museum of handcrafts. The graves of Wagner and his wife had been covered with a huge expanse of ugly concrete (worry about vandals?) and the grave of his loyal dog had been moved off out of the sight of the tourists. May God forgive the government agency who did all this.

almost macho, repeat of bar 17. I find it necessary for musical reasons to begin the return of the music at 17 at the same level of *pp* and slower and more contemplative. Beginning with bar 19 I make a gradual return to the tempi and dynamics heard the first time in this music.

From an educational perspective, during rehearsal this composition represents a wonderful opportunity to discuss harmony with the students and in particular how harmony affects interpretation. To begin with it is difficult to even think of Wagner's music without thinking of its foundation in harmony. But it is also an essential characteristic of German music. When the Netherlands School and the Italian School were so interested in counterpoint, the Germans were far behind still enjoying the vertical joys of music. Even with Bach, though he was an extraordinary master of counterpoint, we are not surprised, that on that famous occasion when he was taken to meet the king at Potsdam for the first time and the court harpsichordist transfixed like others to see the famous Bach enter the room, stopped playing with his hands in mid air, leaving a chord unresolved, that Bach first crossed the room and resolved the chord on the keyboard before turning and allowing himself to be introduced to the king. And that is the power of harmony.

What invests harmony with such power? Certainly there must be a genetic role at work, considering that the overtone series with its powerful organization of harmonic relationships was in place as a natural law of physics and being heard already by all creatures before us who had ears to hear. And for conductors, it is extremely important to remember that you have the feelings of the listeners in your hands and much of the power you hold over their feelings lies in your decisions regarding the role of harmony, both in its linear and vertical employment. And in a composition like this one the decisions by which you convey this harmonic power invests you with profound responsibilities.

Let us consider some examples of the power of harmony employed in linear movement. First, in an example typical of sixteenth-century counterpoint in bar 73 [second bar of the 'coda'] the soprano E♭ is completely at rest until the third beat when the movement in the horn to F *forces* the E♭ to move to D. Similarly, in bar 46 we hear the melody at rest until the F♯

in the horns forces the melody to resume. In my performances I stretch this measure and the length of the F♯ to allow the listeners to feel the pressure of the upward movement.

In several of the cadences of this composition there are some wonderful (musical) examples of the use of 'Placement,' a term often used today by performers of early music. Placement means that the arrival of something is determined not by chronology (the 'correct' time expressed in the notation) but by psychology, or allowing your self to judge when it *feels* like the right time to play.

The most important of these examples is the final cadence. First, there are two vital errors which seem to creep into all editions. The lowest bass note should be a B♭ in the staff in the next to last bar and only drop to below the staff for the final note. The second vital correction which is necessary is that all the woodwind parts in the last two bars which consist of two whole-notes are supposed to be *tied*, they represent a *longa*, a symbol equal to two whole-notes. The over all effect which Wagner had in mind during this cadence is a suspension of time while the listener hears the two separated sounds in the next to last bar, as if they were a great bell or a great choral 'A-men.' But this beautiful effect is lost on the listener unless there is a considerable space between, and after, these two half-notes. In my performances I make each one like a separate bar of dotted half-note and quarter-rest. This is Placement: you conduct the second half-note when it feels right to do so and the final bar as well. Wagner did not write a fermata over the final bar but he would have been the first to agree that the length is again a matter of feeling.

Another perfect example of an appropriate moment for Placement is in bar 11. Here the conductor shows the release on beat 3 of some voices but treats the whole-note as a fermata, allowing him to give the downbeat only later, when it feels right to do so. Any concept of straight time in bars 11 and 12 will greatly minimize the beauty of the arrival of the next *pp* music.

In the role of Placement in bars 15 and 16 we have an interesting case where the conductor's conception of how Wagner heard the principal melody in bar 17 determines the Placement application to bars 15 and 16. If the conductor had concluded that bar 17 should be strong in character then he would prepare the listeners by creating a crescendo in bar 16 to give direction to the added 7th. However it would probably be bad to create a space between bars 16 and 17 as that would produce the effect of an accent on the first note of bar 17 from the perspective of the listener. On the other hand, if the conductor's conception was that Wagner imagined in bar 17 something mysterious, soft and even angelic, then perhaps no crescendo in bar 16 would be appropriate for the added 7th alone would suffice. In this case I would probably make a cut off at the end of bar 16 and then give the downbeat very small and high in the air.

An obvious need for Placement is with regard to the length of bar 71, that is, the conductor only by ear must feel when the music should proceed. Certainly if it is the second time when the music moves forward to the B section ['coda'] then of course one does not make any space where the barline is between bars 71 and 72. The sustained F of bar 71 must connect with the B♭ of bar 72 without pause.

Another occasion where Placement has a great influence on how harmony affects the listener is in bars 43 and 44. Wagner did notate the crescendo in bar 43 but I suspect he imagined it only for the purpose of making the 7th of the chord move forward in time to its resolution in bar 44. In any case Placement becomes an important factor, with regard to the listener, in bar 44 because the more the crescendo in bar 43 then the longer the first half of bar 44 must be. In other words the listener needs enough time to not only perceive the resolution but also time for the music to calm down and to anticipate the *dolce* music at bar 45.

By the way, Wagner did write 'dolce' here, although over bar 45 and not in bar 44 as some editions have it. But what does 'dolce' mean? Certainly we can ignore the dictionary's choice of 'sweet,' if for no other reason because we know how poor language is in describing feeling. When Mozart wrote *dolce* he meant what we mean today if we wrote 'solo' over some voice. In the music of Weber, on the other hand, dolce means 'slower.' Given the association of Weber with this work I think it is a safe bet to imagine that Wagner here meant slower. This allows the conductor to treat these bars *molto rubato* as a singer would.

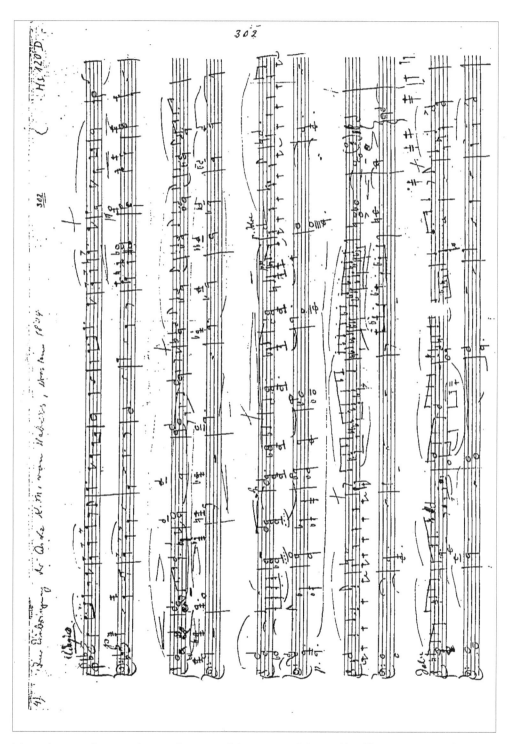

This is the original autograph score, for piano, of the *Trauermusik* for wind band by Wagner. Note that the original conception did not include the introduction music we know today.

This is the first autograph score for the *Trauermusik* by Wagner with designation of the instruments. It is typical of Wagner's autograph large scores that these sweeping slur marks go across the entire page. The intent is that the music is legato, not that it is a literal slur.

Gruss seiner Treuen an Friedrich August

Gruss seiner Treuen an Friedrich August
den Geliebten bei seiner Zuruckkunft aus England den
9. August 1844

COMPOSED:
Summer, 1844, for TTBB, large concert band

SOURCE:
Germany, München, Bayerische Staatsbibliothek Musiksammlung: full score

PUBLICATION:
Dresden, C. F. Meser [1844] for voice and piano
Samtliche Werke, 16, for TTBB only

FIRST PERFORMANCE:
12 August 1844

Together with his court appointment as conductor of the Dresden Liedertafel Choral Society, Wagner had the resonsibility to compose those kinds of occasional pieces which court composers had always written. In the present case, although the autograph score says 'August 9,' it was on 12 August when Wagner and his musicians went to the country palace at Pillnitz to perform this work before Friedrich August II to commemorate his safe return from a journey to England.

Wagner provides a very lengthy and interesting account of the origin and first performance of this composition.

I was to receive the gratification of another triumph in the summer, which, although it was of no particular moment from the musical point of view, was of great social importance. The King of Saxony, towards whom, as I have already said, I had felt warmly drawn when he was Prince Friedrich, was expected home from a long visit to England. The reports received of his stay there had greatly rejoiced my patriotic soul. While this homely monarch, who shrank from all pomp and noisy demonstration, was in England, it happened that the Tsar Nicholas arrived quite unexpectedly on a visit to the Queen. In his honor great festivities and military reviews were held, in which our King, much against military reviews were held, in which our King, much against his will, was obliged to participate, and he was consequently compelled to receive the enthusiastic acclamations of the English crowd, who were most demonstrative in show their preference for him, as compared with the unpopular Tsar. This preference was also reflected in the newspapers, so that a flattering incense floated over from England to our little Saxony which filled us all with a peculiar pride in our King. While I was in this mood, which absorbed me completely, I learned that preparations were being made in Leipzig for a special welcome to the King on his return, which was to be further dignified by a musical festival in the directing of which Mendelssohn was to take part. I made inquiries as to what was going to be done in Dresden, and learned that the King did not propose to call there at all, but was going direct to his summer residence at Pillnitz.

A moment's reflection showed me that this would only further my desire of preparing a pleasant and hearty reception for his Majesty. As I was a servant of the Crown, any attempt on my part to render an act of homage in Dresden might have had the appearance of an official parade which would not be admissible. I seized the idea, therefore, of hurriedly collecting together all who could either play or sing, so that we might perform a Reception song hastily composed in honor of the event. The obstacle to my plan was that my Director Luttichau was away at one of his country seats. To come to an understanding with my colleague Reissiger would, moreover, have involved delay, and given the enterprise the very aspect of an official ovation which I wished to avoid. As no time was to be lost, if anything worthy of the occasion was to be done—as the King was due to arrive in a few days—I availed myself of my position as conductor of the Glee Club, and summoned all its singers and instrumentalists to my aid. In addition to these, I invited the members of our theatrical company, and also those of the orchestra, to join us. This done, I drove quickly to Pillnitz to arrange matters with the Lord Chamberlain, whom I found favorably disposed towards my project. The only leisure I could snatch for composing the verses of my song and setting them to music was during the rapid drive there and back, for by the time I reached home I had to have every thing ready for the copyist and lithographer. The agreeable sensation of rushing through the warm summer air and lovely country, coupled with the sincere affection with which I was inspired for our German Prince, and which had prompted my effort, elated me and worked me up to a high pitch of tension, in which I now formed a clear conception of the lyrical outlines of the *Tannhäuser* March, which first saw the light of day on the occasion of this royal welcome. I soon afterwards developed this theme, and thus produced the march which became the most popular of the melodies I had hitherto composed.

On the next day it had to be tried over with a hundred and twenty instrumentalists and three hundred singers. I had taken the liberty of inviting them to meet me on the stage of the Court Theater, where everything went off capitally. Every one was delighted, and I not the least so, when a messenger arrived from the director, who had just returned to town, requesting an immediate interview. Luttichau was enraged beyond measure at my high-handed proceedings in this matter, of which he had been informed by our good friend Reissiger. If his baronial coronet had been on his head during this interview, it would assuredly have tumbled off. The fact that I should have conducted my negotiations in person with the court officials, and could report that my endeavors had met with extraordinarily prompt success, aroused his deepest fury, for the chief importance of his own position consisted in always representing everything which had to be obtained by these means as surrounded by the greatest obstacles, and hedged in by the strictest etiquette. I offered to cancel everything, but that only embarrassed him the more. I thereupon asked him what he wanted me to do, if the plan was still to be carried out. On this point he seemed uncertain, but thought I had shown a great lack of fellowship in having not only ignored him, but Reissiger as well. I answered that I was perfectly ready to hand over my composition and the conducting of the piece to Reissiger. But he could not swallow this, as he really had an exceedingly poor opinion of Reissiger, of which I was very well aware. His real grievance was that I had arranged the whole business with the Lord Chamberlain, Herr von Reizenstein, who was his personal enemy, and he added that I could form no conception of the rudeness he had been obliged to endure from the hands of this official. This outburst of confidence made it easier for me to exhibit an almost sincere emotion, to which he responded by a shrug of the shoulders, meaning that he must resign himself to a disagreeable necessity.

But my project was even more seriously threatened by the wretched weather than by this storm with the director; for it rained all day in torrents. If it lasted, which it seemed only too likely to do, I could hardly start on the special boat at five o'clock in the morning, as proposed, with my hundreds of musicians, to give an early morning concert at Pillnitz, two hours away. I anticipated such a disaster with genuine dismay. But Rockel consoled me by saying that I could rely upon it that we should have glorious weather the next day; for I was lucky! This belief in my luck has followed me ever since, even down to my latest days; and amid the great misfortunes which have so often hampered my enterprises, I have felt as if this statement were a wicked insult to fate. But this time, at least, my friend was right; the 12th of August, 1844 [sic?] was from sunrise till late at night the most perfect summer day that I can remember in my whole life. The sensation of blissful content with which I saw my light-hearted legion of gaily dressed bandsmen and singers gathering through the auspicious morning mists on board our steamer, swelled my breast with a fervent faith in my lucky star.

By my friendly impetuosity I had succeeded in overcoming Reissiger's smoldering resentment, and had persuaded him to share the honor of our undertaking by conducting the performance of my composition himself. When we arrived at the spot, everything went off splendidly. The King and royal family were visibly touched, and in the evil times that followed the Queen of Saxony spoke of this occasion, I am told, with peculiar emotion, as the fairest day of her life. After Reissiger had wielded his baton with great dignity, and I had sung with the tenors in the choir, we two conductors were summoned to the presence of the royal family. The King warmly expressed his thanks, while the Queen paid us the high compliment of saying that I composed very well and that Reissiger conducted very well. His Majesty asked us to repeat the last three stanzas only, as, owing to a painful ulcerated tooth, he could not remain much longer out of doors. I rapidly devised a combined evolution, the remarkably successful execution of which I am very proud, even to this day. I had the entire song repeated, but, in accordance with the King's wish, only one verse was sung in our original crescent formation. At the beginning of the second verse I made my four hundred undisciplined bandsmen and singers file off in a march through the garden, which, as they gradually receded, was so arranged that the final notes could only reach the royal ear as an echoing dream song.[1]

[1] Richard Wagner, *My Life* (New York: Tudor, 1911), 330ff, 358.

A leading newspaper in Berlin published a note on this performance and gives, perhaps, a more accurate count of the number of performers.

Under the direction of Reissiger & Rich. Wagner, 106 instrumentalists and 200 vocalists went to Pillnitz to serenade the King with a patriotic song composed by Wagner. The King spoke in the most appreciative terms of the excellent piece.[2]

[2] *Berliner Musikalische Zeitung*, 1844, Nr. 1.

A modern edition of this work has been made by Dr. Ronald Johnson, Director of Bands, The University of Northern Iowa.

Huldigungsmarsch (March of Homage)

COMPOSED:
August 1864, for large concert band[1]

SOURCES:
Munich-Wittelsbacher Ausgleichsfonds: full score

PUBLICATION:
Richard Wagner Werke (Leipzig, 1912–1929), xvii
Samtliche Werke (Mainz, 1970), 18/iii (full score)

FIRST PERFORMANCE:
Munich, 5 October 1864

Wagner composed this band composition for the nineteenth birthday of King Ludwig II on 25 August 1864, although not performed until the following 5 October to celebrate his assuming the throne. Of course it was also a celebration of the king's dramatic rescue of Wagner from his financial problems, as he expressed in a poem written in September.

> It was your summons which snatched me from the night that numbed
> my strength in winter's cold …
> Now I tread new paths in pride and joy, in the summer kingdom
> of grace.[2]

Wagner conducted this work himself on several occasions, including one the following year reported by Hans von Bülow.

> Finally last night came the banquet: a big private concert in the Residenztheater with the house brilliantly illuminated, and no audience except His Majesty and between thirty and forty special Wagnerites. Wagner conducted.
> First, the Pilgrims' March from *Tannhäuser*, with a surprise: on the final Eb of the cellos, eighty military band players struck up the *Huldigungs* Marsch behind the scenes. The effect was magnificent, the point of it all being the special relationship between the composer and the King.[3]

[1] A later arrangement for orchestra, published in 1869, was begun by Wagner and finished by Raff.

[2]
> Es war Dein Ruf, der mich der
>   Nacht entrückte,
> die winterlich erstarrt hielt
>   meine Kraft. …
> So wandl' ich stolz beglückt nun
>   neue Pfade
> Im sommerlichen Königreich
>   der Gnade.

[3] Letter of Hans von Bülow to Karl Klindworth, July 13, 1865.

In 1870, Cosima organized a performance of this work as a surprise for Wagner's birthday.

She had devised all kinds of surprises and retained the regimental band, forty-five men strong … At eight o'clock the children, adorned with garlands of roses, burst into Wagner's room, the band struck up the Huldigungsmarsch, and Richard sobbed with delight at the surprise.[4]

4 Richard Count du Moulin-Eckart, *Cosima Wagner*, trans., Catherine Alison Phillips (New York: Knopf, 1931), 1:396ff.

By far the most important performance of this work was for the cornerstone ceremony of the theater in Bayreuth on May 22, 1872, which, of course, was also the composer's birthday. For any one today who knows the Margrave opera house in Bayreuth, one of the most beautiful and ornate Baroque houses in Europe, it seems amazing that Wagner for a time had in mind producing the Ring in this tiny theater. But, upon his visit to the theater, Wagner, of course, found it too small. long period of thought, planning and fundraising had preceded the creation of the Bayreuth Theater. One of the initial musicians who began fundraising was the brilliant young pianist, whom many considered to be the next Liszt, Karl Tausig, 1841–1871. His accidental early death, from a bookcase falling on him, was a great shock to the musicians of Germany and Wagner himself wrote a poem in his honor.

Ripe for Death's harvest,
harvest of Life's last lingering fruit;
ripe all too early,
culled in the flower-fleet springtime of youth:
this thy endeavor, this was thy lot—
thy lot, they endeavor, we cherish and mourn.

For the cornerstone ceremony of the theatre itself the King sent a telegram:

From the profoundest depths of my soul I express to you, dearest friend, my warmest and most sincere congratulations on a day of such significance to all Germany. Blessings and prosperity to the great undertaking next year.

Today more than ever, I am with you in spirit.

Ludwig II

Flags had been set out to mark the outline of the proposed theater and in spite of a rain storm, a crowd gathered to watch the cornerstone being lowered into place as a regimental band played the *Huldigungsmarsch*. Inside the stone was a poem by Wagner:

> O may the secret buried here
> Rest undisturbed for many a year;
> For while it lies beneath this stone,
> The world shall hear its clarion tone.[5]

Wagner then took up the hammer and said, 'Bless you, my stone, long may you stand and firm may you hold!'[6]

Some have pointed out the deep significance, which all present understood, of the performance of the *Huldigungsmarsch*, for without the king's encouragement the world would have never seen this theater, not to mention the completion of the Ring itself.

Wagner had written an oration which he planned to read during these ceremonies, but the rain storm made it necessary to read it instead that evening as part of the continued ceremonies held in the Margrave theater, filled by members of the Margrave's court and Frederick himself. Here trumpets played fanfares based on the principal themes of the Ring, followed by Wagner's speech and finally a performance of Beethoven's *Ninth Symphony* performed by musicians Wagner had hand-picked from throughout Germany. His speech was as follows,

> My Friends and valued Helpers!
> Through you I today am placed in a position surely never occupied before by any artist. You believe in my promise to found for the Germans a Theater of their own, and give me the means to set before you a plain delineation of that theater. For this is to serve, in the first place, the provisional building whose foundation-stone we lay today. When we see each other on this spot once more, that building shall greet you, that building in whose characteristics you will read at once the history of the idea which it embodies. You will find an outer shell constructed of the very simplest material, which at best will remind you of those wooden structures which are knocked together in German towns for gatherings of singers and the like, and pulled down again as soon as the festival is over. How much of this building is reckoned for endurance, shall become clearer to you when you step inside. Here too you will find the very humblest material, a total absence of embellishment; perchance you will be surprised to even miss the cheap adornments with

[5] Hier schliess' ich ein Geheimnis ein,
da ruh' es viele hundert Jahr':
so lange es verwahrt der Stein,
macht es der Welt sich offenbar.

[6] Curt von Westernhagen, *Wagner*, trans., Mary Whittall (Cambridge: Cambridge University Press, 1978), 2:446.

which those wonted festal halls were made attractive to the eye. In the proportions and arrangement of the room and its seats, however, you will find expressed a thought which, once you have grasped it, will place you in a new relation to the play you are about to witness, a relation quite distinct from that in which you had always been involved when visiting our theaters. Should this first impression have proved correct, the mysterious entry of the music will next prepare you for the unveiling and distinct portrayal of scenic pictures that seem to rise from out an ideal world of dreams, and which are meant to set before you the whole reality of a noble art's most skilled illusion. Here at last you are to have no more provisional hints and outlines; so far as lies within the power of the artists of the present the most perfect scenery and miming shall be offered you.

Thus my plan; which bases what I just have called the enduring portion of our edifice on the utmost possible achievement of a sublime illusion. Must I trust myself to lead this artistic exploit to complete success, I take my courage solely from a hope engendered by despair itself. I trust in the German Spirit, and hope for its manifestation in those very regions of our life in which, as our public art, it has languished in the sorriest travesty. Above all I trust in the spirit of German Music, for I know how glad and bright it burns in our musicians so soon as ever a German master wakens it within them; and I trust in our dramatic mimes and singers, for I have learnt that they could be as if transfigured to new life when once a German master led them back from idly playing at a harmful pastime, to true observance of their lofty calling. I trust in our artists, and aloud I dare to say it on a day which, at my simple friendly bidding, has gathered round me so select a host of them from points so distant in our fatherland: when, self-forgetful for very joy in the artwork, they presently shall sound their festal greeting to you with our great Beethoven's wonder-symphony, we all may surely tell ourselves that the work we mean to find today will also be no cheating mirage, though we artists can only vouch for the sincerity of the idea it is to realize.

But to whom shall I turn, to ensure the ideal work its solid lastingness, the stage its monumental shrine?

Of late our undertaking has often been styled the erection of a 'National theater at Bayreuth.' I have no authority to accept that title. Where is the 'nation,' to erect itself this theater? When the French National Assembly was dealing with the State-subvention of the great Parisian theaters a little while ago, each speaker warmly advocated the continuance, nay, the increase of their subsidies, since the maintenance of these theaters was a debt not merely due to France, but to Europe which had accustomed itself to receiving from them its laws of intellectual culture. Can we imagine the embarrassment, the perplexity into which a German parliament would fall, had it to handle a similar question? The debates perhaps would terminate in the comforting conclusion that our theaters required no national support at all, since the French National Assembly had already provided for *their* needs too.

In the best event our theater would be treated as the German Reich was treated in our various Landtags but a few years back: namely, as a pure chimera.

Though a vision of the true German Theater has built itself before my mental eye, I have had to promptly recognize that I should be abandoned from both within and without, were I to step before the nation with that scheme. Yet I may be told that, though one man might not be believed, the word of many would perhaps find credence: that one really might succeed in floating a gigantic limited company, to commission an architect to rear a sumptuous fabric somewhere or other, which one then might dub a 'German National Theater' in full confidence that a German-national theatric art would spring up in it of itself. All the world now pins its faith to a continual, and in our latter days an extremely rapid 'progress,' without any clear idea of what we are advancing towards, or the kind of step we are marching; but those who brought a really new thing to the world have never been asked what relation they bore to this 'progressive' surrounding, that met them with naught but obstacles and opposition. On a holiday like this we will not recall the undisguised complaints, the deep despair of our very greatest minds, whose labors showed the only veritable progress; but perhaps you will allow the man you honor today with so unusual a distinction, to express his heartfelt joy that the thought of a single individual has been understood and embraced in his lifetime by so large a number of friends as your gathering here and now attests.

I had only you, the friends of my peculiar art, my deeds and labors, for sympathizers with my projects: only asking your assistance for my work, could I approach you. To be able to set that work intact and pure before those who have shown their serious liking for my art in spite of all adulteration and defacement—this was my wish; to you I could impart it sans presumption. And solely in this almost personal relation to you, my friends and helpers, can I see the present ground on which to lay the stone to bear the whole ambitious edifice of our noblest German hopes. Though it be but a provisional one, in that it will resemble all of German's outward Form for centuries. 'Tis the essence of the German spirit, to build from within: the eternal God lives in him, of a truth, before he builds a temple to His glory. And that temple will proclaim the inner spirit to the outer eye in measure and that spirit has matured its amplest individuality. So I will call this stone the talisman whose power shall unseal to you the hidden secrets of that spirit. Let it now but bear the scaffolding whose help we need for that Illusion which shall clear for you life's truest mirror, and already it is firmly, truly laid to bear the prouder edifice whene'er the German Folk desires, in its own honor, to enter its possession with you. So be it consecrated by your love, your blessings, the gratitude I bear you, all of you, who have sped, enheartened, given to and helped me! Be it consecrated by the spirit that inspired you to hear my call; that filled you with the courage, taunts unheeding, to trust me wholly; that found in me a voice to call you, because it dared to hope to recognize itself within your hearts: the German Spirit, that shouts to you across the centuries it every young Good-morrow.

Some anti-Wagner newspapers gave a somewhat nasty aftertaste to this ceremony. A paper in Leipzig, for example, wrote, 'We consider it a farce … Many of the scenes that occurred there are simply nauseating.'[7]

I previously owned original first editions of piano arrangements of this work by both Hans von Bülow and by Wagner himself. The Wagner arrangement is especially interesting, as one might imagine it reflects how the composer himself might play it on the piano. It has some effective differences with the band version. In the first fast tempo, for example, the triplet figure is doubled up, so that it occurs on both the second and fourth beat which gives considerably more drive to the movement. Also the very long tone (four bars of tied whole-notes) near the end is here given some movement.[8]

A final note on performance practice should be mentioned. I find in modern performances I have heard that many conductors are unaware of a long tradition, dating from the Baroque, in which it was expected that the opening music would be understood to be a *Largo*. The fast tempo does not begin until the *alle breve* time appears.

[7] Henry T. Finck, *Wagner and his Works* (New York: Greenwood Press, 1968), 2:274.

[8] The modern edition of this work, which incorporates these changes, is available from <www.whitwellbooks.com>.

'Elsa's Procession to the Cathedral'

'Elsa's Procession to the Cathedral'
(*Lohengrin*, act 2, scene 4)

We include this well-known 'band' composition, for it very nearly is a band work. It begins as a composition for wind band, which after 32 bars is joined by a unison violin melody and eventually two male choirs. These two male choirs function antiphonally, thereby giving the effect of a composition for three ensembles. It is inexplicable why the arrangement played by bands in America leaves out one of the male choirs, and of course a vital part of the logic.[1]

We also wanted to include this brief discussion of 'Elsa,' in order to bring to the reader's attention an extensive description by Wagner of the very scene in the opera when this music is played. His description, in a letter of 31 October 1853, is unusually vivid and perhaps will shed light for those who play this music.

[1] My modern edition available through <www.whitwellbooks.com> uses *all* the music.

> You think that my stage arrangement is inadequate to represent Elsa's bridal procession in the second act in conformity with the length of the music (as well as with the artistic effect I intended), and you suggest a courtly ceremony—as prelude to the actual bridal procession—with which I cannot agree at all. That is much too much ceremonial for the noble, naive simplicity of that time … The particular atmosphere which my *Lohengrin* should produce is that here we see before us an ancient *German* kingdom in its finest, most ideal aspect. Here no one does anything out of mere routine and court custom, but in every encounter the participants take a direct and genuinely personal part; here there is no despotic pomp which has its 'bodyguards' (oh! oh!) and orders the 'people pushed back' to form a 'lane' for the high nobility … I beg of you, for God's sake, take out that awful stuff with the masters of ceremonies, marshals, bodyguards, etc.: they must have no further place *here*. Let my *Lohengrin* be beautiful, but not ostentatious …
>
> Elsa must—on the high ground before the palace—actually come to a stop. She is moved and affected, as if overcome by bliss. Only after 8 measures does she once more proceed very slowly toward the cathedral, sometimes, pausing, cordially and naively acknowledging greet-

ings. Not only does it take shape *this way*, but it actually becomes what I intended it to be; namely, no marchlike procession, but the infinitely significant advance of Elsa to the altar.

I know you'll understand me now, and would have understood me right away if I had played over the music to you.[2]

[2] John N. Burk, *Letters of Richard Wagner* (New York: Vienna House, 1972), 333ff.

Wagner himself seemed quite moved by this music, as we see in a similar letter to Theodor Uhlig in Dresden, written from Zurich on 28 December 1851.

Right at the beginning of the second scene of this same act—Elsa's appearance on the balcony—in the woodwind prelude—it struck me that a motif is heard here for the first time in the 7th, 8th and 9th bars of Elsa's nocturnal appearance, which is later developed, and broadly and brilliantly executed, when, in broad daylight and in all her glory, Elsa makes her way to church. I realized from this that the themes that I write always originate in the context of, and according to the character of, some visual phenomenon on stage.[3]

3 Ibid., 242.

Fanfares

FANFAREN FUR 4 SIGNAL TROMPETEN

This work consists of three fanfares for four natural trumpets and timpani, and is dedicated to the Bavarian King's 6th Chevaulegers-Regiment. References to fanfares appear occasionally in Wagner's correspondence which may reflect an occasion when these may have been used. For example, in a letter to Ludwig II in 1875 Wagner is recounting an outdoor reception and he mentions 'I then bade the trumpeter call my guests together.'[1, 2]

[1] In John N. Burk, *Letters of Richard Wagner* (New York: Vienna House, 1972), 849.

[2] The score and parts of the four fanfares are available from <www.whitwellbooks.com>.

RING FANFARES

In the Marine Band Library, Washington, DC, is a photocopy of a page of sketches, said to be brass fanfares performed at the time of the first production of the Ring in Bayreuth. The present writer found this page to probably be just the original sketches for the fanfares and in any case is very difficult to read, but it appears to be simple quotations of now-familiar motives of the Ring.

Kaisermarsch

COMPOSED:
Early 1871

PUBLICATION (FOR ORCHESTRA):
Richard Wagner Werke (Leipzig, 1912–1929), xviii
Samtliche Werke (Mainz, 1970), 18/iii

Wagner was moved by the successes of the German armies in the 1870–1871 War and for the return of the troops to Berlin he proposed composing a march for military band, with a choral finale which would be sung by soldiers and perhaps joined by the audience. He completed a rough draft on 16 March 1871.[1]

When Berlin showed no interest in a patriotic work, Wagner turned the idea into one for orchestra. According to his wife, Wagner had difficulty writing the work and was angry and full of disgust.

> I cannot do a thing of this sort when no ideas suggest themselves in connection with it, and if I do think of something, there is no end to it. A march is an absurd affair. At most it can only be a people's song, yet at the same time it is not intended to be sung; it is nonsensical. But I must have my great thread, on which I develop my music. I can do nothing in this way.[2]

Wagner conducted the Berlin premiere on 5 May 1871, at a concert in the presence of Emperor Wilhelm I. He conducted the work again in Albert Hall, London, but he was by then older, very tired, and experienced memory slips.[3]

[1] Joachim Bergfeld, ed., *The Diary of Richard Wagner* (Cambridge: Cambridge University Press, 1980), 186, and Henry T. Finck, *Wagner and his Works* (New York: Greenwood Press, 1968), 2:125. A poem Wagner wrote which would form the words for the choral part he had sent in a copy to Bismarck in January, 1871. The poem can be found in Bergfeld, 187.

[2] Richard Count du Moulin-Eckart, *Cosima Wagner*, trans., Catherine Alison Phillips (New York: Alfred, 1931), 2:471ff.

[3] Adolphe Jullien, *Richard Wagner* (Neptune, NJ: Paganiniana, 1981), 329.

Hunting Chorus

SCORED:
Early 1839, for 12 horns and voices.

SOURCE:
Stanford University, CA, Green Library, Department of Special Collections: manuscript

PUBLICATION:
Samtliche Werke (Mainz, 1970), 20/iii

This is an arrangement Wagner made of the 'Hunting Chorus' from Weber's *Euryanthe*.

Authorized Arrangements

During the latter part of the nineteenth century, the Hanover publisher, Louis Oertel, who specialized in band music, published a fifteen-minute band transcription of the 'Brunhilde's Awakening' scene from *Siegfried*. This publication is of interest because of the text at the beginning which tells us 'arranged by Anton Seidl and Gottfried Sonntag under the supervision (Aufsicht) of the Master.' The text continues,

> This composition was arranged, with the approval and under the supervision of Richard Wagner, for the band of the 7th Bavarian Infanterie-Regiment, by Anton Seidl and Gottfried Sonntag ('Kg. Rechnungsrat a.D. in Bayreuth'). The new instrumentation [of this published version] was done by Oskar Junger, Kg. Obermusikmeister, 7th Bavarian Infanterie-Regiment 'Prinz Leopold' in Bayreuth.

This introductory text also includes an excerpt from a letter of Seidl to Sonntag which suggests that the original arrangement can be dated in 1878.

Of course our principal interest lies with the nature of the 'supervision' by Wagner. The fact that this transcription was done for a regimental band stationed at Bayreuth adds weight to this possibility of some participation by Wagner. So does the involvement of Anton Seidl, later a famous Wagnerian conductor, but at this time a copyist and disciple of Wagner.

The question is complicated by the fact that Oertel published not the Seidl-Sonntag-Wagner version, but a later one revised by Junger. Further, this score is only a three-stave condensed score with no list of the complete instrumentation—therefore, whatever set of parts one has, one is never completely sure if everything is complete.

As of this date, the present writer doubts that it will ever be possible to learn much more about Wagner's personal relationship to this transcription.

Another Seidl, unrelated to Anton, was responsible for three lengthy band transcriptions from the Ring which were published by Schott during the 1880s. This was Arthur Seidel, conductor and composer, who was born 13 April 1849 in Neisse and died 28 March 1910 in Breslau.

During the latter part of his life, Wagner accepted monies in advance from Schott with the promise of giving them future works to publish.[1] The present writer was told, while visiting the publisher in Mainz in 1977, that the engagement of Seidel to prepare the Ring band arrangements was an attempt on the part of the publisher to recoup some of the monies given the composer. The understanding at Schott, in 1977, was that Seidel had done these arrangements from the actual autograph scores, which disappeared during World War II. This seems reasonable, as the band scores (but not parts) were undoubtedly published before the orchestral score and parts.

Seidel prepared a 'Fantasie,' on *Die Walküre*, *Siegfried*, and *Das Götterdämmerung*, each consisting of twenty minutes, or more, of non-stop music. Seidel had earlier published projects of this nature, but they tend to be traditional 'pot-pourri' works consisting of rapidly changing excerpts and melodies. What makes the Ring Fantasies so much more successful is that they consist of much lengthy segments. On the other hand, in the opinion of the present writer, each of the Fantasies contains about fifteen-minutes of beautiful, inspired transcription, with the rest suffering from awkward modulations, weak connection points, and some scoring which just doesn't sound well.

But this is not to detract from Seidel's accomplishment: he was making band transcriptions of music no one had ever heard and within these vast operatic scores he certainly found the right passages to transcribe. We must also credit Schott, whose aesthetic ideals prompted them to publish these gigantic band scores at a time when German military bands were already traveling full speed on their long decline down to the lowest popular repertoire.

Several large band libraries in the United States own copies of the Seidel transcriptions, including the Marine Band, Eastman School of Music, and the University of Illinois.

[1] Wagner confirms this arrangement in his *My Life*, 803.

My frustration with the uneven quality of the Seidel transcriptions led me in the Summer of 1988 to spend four months making my own band transcriptions of excerpts of music from the *Ring*.[2]

[2] These will be available at <www.whitwellbooks.com>, where one can also see sample scores and hear recordings.

About the Author

Dr. David Whitwell is a graduate ('with distinction') of the University of Michigan and the Catholic University of America, Washington DC (PhD, Musicology, Distinguished Alumni Award, 2000) and has studied conducting with Eugene Ormandy and at the Akademie fur Musik, Vienna. Prior to coming to Northridge, Dr. Whitwell participated in concerts throughout the United States and Asia as Associate First Horn in the USAF Band and Orchestra in Washington DC, and in recitals throughout South America in cooperation with the United States State Department.

At the California State University, Northridge, which is in Los Angeles, Dr. Whitwell developed the CSUN Wind Ensemble into an ensemble of international reputation, with international tours to Europe in 1981 and 1989 and to Japan in 1984. The CSUN Wind Ensemble has made professional studio recordings for BBC (London), the Koln Westdeutscher Rundfunk (Germany), NOS National Radio (The Netherlands), Zurich Radio (Switzerland), the Television Broadcasting System (Japan) as well as for the United States State Department for broadcast on its 'Voice of America' program. The CSUN Wind Ensemble's recording with the Mirecourt Trio in 1982 was named the 'Record of the Year' by The Village Voice. Composers who have guest conducted Whitwell's ensembles include Aaron Copland, Ernest Krenek, Alan Hovhaness, Morton Gould, Karel Husa, Frank Erickson and Vaclav Nelhybel.

Dr. Whitwell has been a guest professor in 100 different universities and conservatories throughout the United States and in 23 foreign countries (most recently in China, in an elite school housed in the Forbidden City). Guest conducting experiences have included the Philadelphia Orchestra, Seattle Symphony Orchestra, the Czech Radio Orchestras of Brno and Bratislava, The National Youth Orchestra of Israel, as well as resident wind ensembles in Russia, Israel, Austria, Switzerland, Germany, England, Wales, The Netherlands, Portugal, Peru, Korea, Japan, Taiwan, Canada and the United States.

He is a past president of the College Band Directors National Association, a member of the Präsidium of the International Society for the Promotion of Band Music, and was a member of the founding board of directors of the World Association for Symphonic Bands and Ensembles (WASBE). In 1964 he was made an honorary life member of Kappa Kappa Psi, a national professional music fraternity. In September, 2001, he was a delegate to the UNESCO Conference on Global Music in Tokyo. He has been knighted by sovereign organizations in France, Portugal and Scotland and has been awarded the gold medal of Kerkrade, The Netherlands, and the silver medal of Wangen, Germany, the highest honor given wind conductors in the United States, the medal of the Academy of Wind and Percussion Arts (National Band Association) and the highest honor given wind conductors in Austria, the gold medal of the Austrian Band Association. He is a member of the Hall of Fame of the California Music Educators Association.

Dr. Whitwell's publications include more than 127 articles on wind literature including publications in Music and Letters (London), the London Musical Times, the Mozart-Jahrbuch (Salzburg), and 39 books, among which is his 13-volume *History and Literature of the Wind Band and Wind Ensemble* and an 8-volume series on *Aesthetics in Music*. In addition to numerous modern editions of early wind band music his original compositions include 5 symphonies.

David Whitwell was named as one of six men who have determined the course of American bands during the second half of the 20th century, in the definitive history, *The Twentieth Century American Wind Band* (Meredith Music).

A doctoral dissertation by German Gonzales (2007, Arizona State University) is dedicated to the life and conducting career of David Whitwell through the year 1977. David Whitwell is one of nine men described by Paula A. Crider in *The Conductor's Legacy* (Chicago: GIA, 2010) as 'the legendary conductors' of the 20th century.

'I can't imagine the 2nd half of the 20th century—without David Whitwell and what he has given to all of the rest of us.' Frederick Fennell (1993)

CPSIA information can be obtained
at www.ICGtesting.com
Printed in the USA
BVHW010814210819
556411BV00002B/39/P